Life is not a
STRESS
REHEARSAL

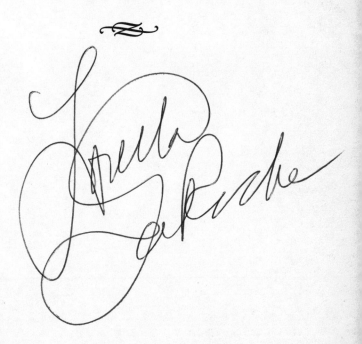

ALSO BY LORETTA LAROCHE

Relax! You May Only Have a Few Minutes Left

Francesca, the Inner Grandmother

Broadway Books   New York

Life is not a STRESS REHEARSAL

*Bringing Yesterday's Sane Wisdom
into Today's Insane World*

Loretta LaRoche

BROADWAY

LIFE IS NOT A STRESS REHEARSAL. Copyright © 2001 by Loretta LaRoche.
All rights reserved. No part of this book may be reproduced or transmitted
in any form or by any means, electronic or mechanical, including
photocopying, recording, or by any information storage and retrieval
system, without written permission from the publisher. For information,
address Broadway Books, a division of Random House, Inc., 1540
Broadway, New York, NY 10036.

Broadway Books titles may be purchased for business or promotional use or
for special sales. For information, please write to: Special Markets
Department, Random House, Inc., 1540 Broadway, New York, NY 10036.

PRINTED IN THE UNITED STATES OF AMERICA

BROADWAY BOOKS and its logo, a letter B bisected on the diagonal, are
trademarks of Broadway Books, a division of Random House, Inc.

Visit our website at www.broadwaybooks.com

First trade paperback edition published 2002

Designed by Lisa Sloane

The Library of Congress has cataloged the hardcover edition as follows:

LaRoche, Loretta, 1939–
Life is not a stress rehearsal: bringing yesterday's sane wisdom into today's
insane world / Loretta LaRoche.—1st ed.
p. cm.
1. Stress (Psychology)—Prevention. 2. Conduct of life. I. Title.
BF575.S75 .L275 2001
155.9'042—dc21
00-065188

ISBN 0-7679-0666-7

1 3 5 7 9 10 8 6 4 2

To my grandmother, Francesca Arico,
who said, "Never forget me," and I never will.
You are always with me . . .

Acknowledgments

MANY THANKS to my literary agent Brian DeFiore, a dear friend and collaborator in all good things; to Lauren Marino, Beth Dickey, Gerry Howard, Catherine Pollock, of Broadway Books, you are dream makers; to Tricia Zuttermeister for her research; to Susan Cohen for her understanding and wisdom; to my children: Erik, my business partner, who makes almost everything possible, to Laurie, for her intense humor and survival skills, to Jon, the oldest, for his grace and dignity; to my mother, for her ability to still see absurdity at ninety; to my husband Bob for his ability to endure living with a wacky wild woman; to PBS, in particular WGBH Boston, and my mentor Laurie Donnelly, for giving me the opportunity to be on national television; and to all the many people who have attended my lectures, you have allowed me the gift of being myself.

Contents

Listening to the Inner Grandmother

On the death of the obvious

HERE'S WHAT GOES on in a typical day in the life of a person in America at the beginning of the 21st century:

We wake up, probably in a room that has some sort of electronic climate control and closed windows, because who would dare take the risk that we might get an unscheduled breeze in the middle of the night? We wander into the bathroom to brush our teeth: we have four different brands of toothpaste to choose from, one for whitening, one with fluoride protection, one for fresher breath, and one that's 100% organic and natural. We floss, we water-pick, we sandpaper our teeth to the stubs.

Then we take a shower. Our shower head is able to pulsate, vibrate, and gyrate; it can probably even fill in if we need an extra blender. Keep in mind that "multi-tasking" is very important in today's world, so if we can wash our backs and make our breakfast smoothie at the same time, we're golden.

We have a natural soap, a cleansing soap, a moisturizing soap, and an astringent soap. We have soaps that smell like chrysanthemum, rose petals, and lily-of-the-valley; like basil, rosemary, parsley, and avocado. Just choosing the soap we use to wash behind our ears is like picking a week's worth of groceries from the farmer's market. Are we washing our face, or making a marinara sauce?

Next, we wash our hair. We don't use shampoo, no. We use a hair care system. First a pre-wash with a clarifying treatment, then a reconstructor, then a conditioner, then— depending on the weather—we choose either a volumizer or a curl enhancer.

We reach for the deodorant, but then remember a television show we saw yesterday that warned us that a new scientific study has determined that when rats are exposed to an amount of deodorant roughly equivalent to the highest peak of Mount Everest, they develop a pre-cancerous condition.

We haven't even left the bathroom and we've used fifteen products, made twenty decisions, had a mild case of panic about our susceptibility to a debilitating disease, and probably feel awful about ourselves because someone who needs so much help can't possibly be good enough to go out into the world. All we want to do is go back to sleep.

But we can't: we all know that in today's world, "if you snooze, you lose," so we get up, we get dressed, we get ready. We go down to breakfast.

We open the refrigerator, dig around in the plastic meat bin looking for some bacon to fry—memories of the delicious smell and fabulous taste of the crisp meat making our mouths water. Then we hear the voice in our head of the low-fat nazi: "You're eating WHAT? Do you know how many calories that has? Do you know how much saturated fat? You can't eat that! You should be ashamed of yourself for even *thinking* of that."

So, we skip the bacon. Instead we just grab for two eggs, and we're about to crack them into the pan when, this time, it's the cholesterol police: "Didn't your doctor tell you your level was on the high end of the middle range? Don't eat that! You're asking for trouble."

So we grab a piece of no-fat, high-fiber, twelve-grain bread, and we toast it, and eat it, dry, of course. No butter. It feels like we're munching on tree bark. Every bit of moisture in our body starts surging to our mouth and gets sucked into our cheeks to save us from the drought. That's breakfast. With, of course, a few vitamin supplements washed down with bottled mineral water.

Let's say it's a weekend, not even a workday. We have errands to run, we want to go to the supermarket.

It's a beautiful sunny day, so we lather ourselves with sun block containing SFP45 for the fifteen seconds when we're between the car and the store because, well, you can't be too careful about ultraviolet rays.

In the car we turn on the radio, and we listen to a call-in show in which we hear a woman caller being told she may well have a martyr complex because she chose to eat tree bark for breakfast instead of just having the piece of bacon she craved.

We switch stations, and listen to another call-in show where the caller is told that she may have an eating disorder because she just keeps giving in to her craving for bacon. Has she tried tree bark instead?

We go to the supermarket, and we turn on our cellular phone, hook up our pager, access the shopping list we've downloaded into our palm pilot; we now look more like a member of a swat team than someone shopping for groceries. But God forbid we should be out of touch for ten minutes in case something critical happens. And, since we have the contraptions there with us—what the hell, we call home and tell everyone we got bread.

We get the groceries home, and then we start a trauma unit in our kitchen, pulling on our rubber gloves, scrubbing every surface with disinfectant, keeping children under the age of eighteen out of the line of fire, as we open the package of chicken. After all, you can never be too careful when it comes to chicken.

And do we dare wash it with water from the tap? That's just as unhealthy. No, we wash the chicken with Evian.

Let's face it. We've gone mad.

I've been working in the field of wellness and stress reduction for thirty years, trying to help people relieve the effects of stress in their lives, and I've done it with the help of my own innate sense of the absurd. I see life as funny. I always have.

Call me crazy (and believe me, many people have), but I think that what most of us do in the course of a normal day is more ridiculous and hilarious than any episode of Seinfeld. I mean, really. Think about it! Think about the number of choices and the minutiae and the fear and the insecurity that we all have to face just to get through the day.

Look closely at what's going on today: as a nation we spend 9.3 billion dollars a year on stress management. 9.3 BILLION! And is it really because we're living in a time that is so much more difficult than for the generations that came before us? Generations that were faced with World Wars, extreme poverty, sexual and racial intolerance, and unfair access to education?

Are we stressed out because we face real life-threatening situations day-in and day-out, or is it because we have become a nation of individuals who have lost touch with reality and the things that are really important?

It seems to me that the quickened pace, the media images, the technology of immediacy, and the pressure of nonstop marketing has eclipsed rational thinking and common sense. I think we're suffering from the **death of the obvious.**

I spend a big part of my time these days helping people relieve stress by getting in touch with their own clear vision of common sense: by helping them to see just how absurd and needlessly complex and stressful the details of our lives have become.

What I long for, and what I think most people long for, is a return to sanity. And over the last several years we've seen that craving manifest itself in the "simplicity" movement, and in what some people call the "return to spirituality."

People look in different places. But it seems to me that in a way, what we're all looking for is a way to live the life that people lived fifty or sixty years ago. Despite the fact that for many people it seems almost pandemic to suggest this, our grandparents' generation was a lot saner than ours is today. It was more in touch and more involved with friends, family, and community.

Is it possible to go back? Of course not. No one is going to go back to the days before cordless phones or exercise classes or television or e-mail. And, in fact, to think that the lives our grandparents lived was better than ours is a little naïve. There was terrible hardship and poverty for much of that generation. Their lives were smaller in scope, and their possibilities narrower.

Still, I think there are lessons to be learned from yesterday's lifestyle. A great deal of what I am going to try to accomplish in this book is to try to find the balance between the possibilities of today's world and the sanity of yesterday's.

Speaking of sanity, I find it fascinating, and more than a little encouraging, that a new movement has been shaking up the ranks of psychology. Called "positive psychology," and led by Dr. Martin Seligman, author of *Learned Optimism*, it proposes the idea that professionals should be paying more attention to what's *right* with their patients than what's wrong with them.

This movement makes the case that ever since Freud, the disciplines of psychology and psychiatry have shortsightedly focussed on illness and dysfunction—on helping patients to recover from, or "cope with" their weaknesses. Seligman and his followers think that this current practice—the treating of people with psychological disorders such as depression, anxiety, schizophrenia and the like—is only one part of what psychology should be examining. The area that psychology has been ignoring, and that could have a more powerful and beneficial effect on the human race, is the study of the human strengths, such as optimism, resiliency, hope, love, joy, originality, good parenting, civility, altruism, and moderation.

They believe that psychology should grow to encompass the study of virtue and human strengths, not just weakness and dysfunction.

I applaud Dr. Seligman and the people who are working toward developing this science. We're a society that is obsessed with paying attention to the negative and to dysfunction; on coping with how awful life is rather than on learning how to enjoy, and celebrate, how wonderful it is.

But I also find myself laughing, because when I think of the millions of dollars being spent to convince people that this is a worthy pursuit, I step back for a moment and think, "Wait a minute! My grandmother knew this stuff!" Nobody had to tell the people of my grandparents' generation that the way to live a contented and fulfilled life was to focus on things like moderation, altruism, connection, humor, originality and civility. These things were a given for their generation. These values were taught by society, and people lived by them, often instinctively, or if not, by sheer parental force.

I want us to think about why these qualities seemed so much more important to our grandparents' generation than they do to ours. And I want us to think about what we can do to clear the clutter out of our lives and bring back what's important.

It's so sad that today, the qualities we see being honored in the mass media are often the opposite of our grandparents' values. Think about it: aggressiveness, ennui, rudeness, impatience, self-entitlement, narcissism. Aren't those the qualities we see over and over in the media, personified by the celebrities who become famous and revered in our society?

We live in a time full of amazing promise and opportunity, a time when the entire world is open for us to explore. Creativity and communication and adventure and even FUN could be the center points of rich and rewarding lives. But the stresses and the over-stimulation, the hype and the exhaustive nature of so much of today's lifestyle throws so many of us out of whack. We stop seeing the potential for wonder around us and only see the demands for our resources. Sometimes even the things we think might be the answer, like "simplifying" or "spirituality," become further demands that make us feel still more inadequate and therefore more stressed.

The trick is to see the inauthenticity of what is being presented to us. So many of the elements of today's lifestyle are psychologically harmful: we're offered quick fixes and consumer goods as a way to assuage and cover up our feeling of emptiness.

We used to walk home after work to find the house filled with delicious aromas, and with other people waiting there, happy to see us. Now, that's a distant memory. The closest we get is watching television ads that show people using a new hair gel that makes them happy. Dogs are leaping in the air, the sun is shining, and big happy families are gathered in front of pristine homes and manicured lawns, sharing their joy over the new Dodge Durango.

Kalle Lasn, a Canadian activist, believes that "young people have been stewed from birth in an unprecedented marinade of advertising." And that leads to us all suffering from "possession obsession." We truly believe that there are products that can make us happy.

The things that were important to my grandparents' generation more clearly resembled the values of "positive psychology." Everything was done in moderation and with a certain degree of bemused skepticism. My grandmother would never have bought a bottled marinara sauce just because it had a photo of a nice-looking Italian woman on the label holding a wooden spoon, or because it came from an exclusive gourmet shop. She would have laughed at it, said "no thank you," and have gone on to make what she knew was her own far superior sauce. Her self-esteem wasn't tied into buying an expensive product. *She was the product!*

If we could all just take a step back and take the time to think about the absurdity of so much of what we have let infiltrate our lives, and how it leads to stress, anger, pain and impotent longing, we might feel lighter of spirit, more joyful, and spiritually richer.

If we exchange my grandmother's bemused skepticism for modern day euphemisms, we might get something called "the big DUH!"—a term I learned from one of my grandkids. You know what a "duh" is? It's something so obvious that, from a kid's point of view, you're pretty dumb if you don't understand it already. It's got a silent ring of derision, as if you added the term "you jerk" at the end, but of course, you don't have to.

> WHY DO YOU SUPPOSE WE HAVE PEOPLE KILLING EACH OTHER DUE TO ROAD RAGE NOW? IN THE YEAR 2000? WHEN CARS ARE AIR CONDITIONED AND HAVE COMPACT DISC PLAYERS AND TELEPHONES? AND NOT IN OUR GRANDPARENTS' GENERATION WHEN THEY WENT 40 MPH, AND ENDED UP BROKEN DOWN ON THE SIDE OF THE ROAD NINE TIMES OUT OF TEN?

I think the first time I heard the phrase was when I took two of my grandchildren to the movies. During a particularly tense scene, when a character was walking through a dark empty house at night or something like that, the six-year-old whispered over to me and to the nine-year-old: "something bad is going to happen," and the nine-year-old said back to him: "Well, duh!"

Now, maybe it's just me (I've been told that I have a somewhat unique perspective on the world), but I think a lot of the nonsense I see around me, and a lot of the things that cause people inordinate amounts of stress in their lives, are big "duh's."

Why, for example, is there such an enormous amount of rage? There is road rage, air rage, cyber rage, gender rage, inner city rage, supermarket rage. It feels like everyone is pissed off at someone or something. One of my favorite rage stories comes from the Internet. It has to do with flight delays that occurred during some very bad weather in Chicago. There was a long line of people waiting to be rebooked, and the gate agent was doing her best to attend to everyone's needs. Most of the customers were patiently waiting their turn. But I guess there's always someone who refuses to believe that flying in a thunderstorm is not the wisest thing.

A gentleman pushed his way to the front of the line and stated that he simply had to get on the next flight because he had an important meeting to attend. The agent politely explained that he had to wait his turn, that there were a lot of people in front of him. He kept insisting and then finally asked, in a very pompous tone of voice "do you know who I am?"

The agent grabbed her microphone and announced to the crowd: "Attention! Attention! Does anyone here know who this man is? He seems to have lost his identity!" The man was insulted and immediately countered with "Well, screw you." She responded," Sir, you'll have to get to the back of the line to do that, too. There are a lot of people ahead of you!"

The whole crowd burst into applause. Now, of course we realize that this sort of sarcasm could put the airline out of business pretty fast, but the applause from the crowd proves that people are excited when arrogance is not rewarded. And isn't that what a lot of the rage is about? Arrogance, self-entitlement, a low threshold of frustration? They've all grown out of a society in which we want all our demands attended to IMMEDIATELY.

It's like so many of us have turned into the toddler who can only think and say "Me want candy NOW," including the tendency to throw tantrums. In my grandmother's generation, kids were met with raised eyebrows from their parents, and they knew that they'd better back down. My own mother used to say "Just who do you think you are?" and if that didn't work, the good sisters of Saint Joseph were there to report your misbehavior to God. That kept people feeling humble. Humility can sometimes keep rage in check.

But if being humble doesn't click for you, then let me give you a good dose of fear. Everytime you get enraged, your blood pressure goes up, your heart rate escalates, your body becomes extremely tense. You could even have a heart attack or stroke. You put yourself at the risk of major injury or death, because someone has gotten one car length ahead of you, or because someone at the supermarket has nine items in the eight item checkout line. This is a big "duh."

Yes, I'm being irreverent, and believe me I realize it's not that simple. However, if you can take a step back and really do some critical thinking, you can begin to see another point of view. No matter how big a rush you're in, no matter how long you've waited in traffic, banging your head against the windshield is stupid. Do you know what my grandmother would have said? "Stunata!" which translates to "the lights are on, but nobody's home."

Here's a quick bit of advice: when you feel yourself getting **enraged**, try instead to **engage**. Engage your rational mind by asking yourself "what's the point of this outburst?" Take a step back. Your irrational mind would like you to act out an entire episode of *Chicago Hope*, because it makes you feel important. But let's face it, not everything is an emergency! Instead of giving into the rage, really think about what you're doing, and remember how silly enraged behavior really is, most of the time. When is the last time you saw someone really acting out in fury? Was it a pretty sight?

⮑

What I want to accomplish with this book is to point out the absurdity. I want us all to take a step back and look at some of the things we do today through our grandmothers' eyes. I want us to all learn to think about how the values that were important to that generation can be used as a filter against the stuff that can make our lives so difficult.

I think there's something inherently absurd about our society today, something that's filling us all with stress and rage and anger, and the first step toward helping ourselves out of the mess we find ourselves in is simply to start to notice. We have to stop buying into the things that we now consider normal, but that our grandparents would have thought were insane. We have to see the big "duh's."

I am helped to see the "duh's" by thinking of my grandparents, and in particular my grandmother Francesca. I often carry around a picture of her in my head and think, "What would Francesca have said about this?" (Often the answer is "have a little meatball, you'll feel better.")

My grandmother, a first-generation Italian, lived in a loud, bustling neighborhood in Brooklyn in which the doors were always open and the kitchen was always full. But she was quite prim and proper. Her values and her sensibility were almost puritan—if it wasn't for the smell of spaghetti sauce that always infused the house, she could have been the Queen of England! (In fact, my grandfather used to call her "la Regina"—the Queen.)

It was important to her to always do the "right" thing, the "proper" thing. She cared a lot about what other people thought of her family. She made sure that her children were well dressed, well groomed, spoke politely and had impeccable manners.

And she loved to cook! She loved to stuff everyone and everything. Cooking was her creative outlet. She'd go to the store—which was a place not only to do the marketing, but to gossip with the shopkeepers and the other neighbors—and depending on what looked good to her that day, she'd devise a menu. She needed to be creative, because there was not a lot of money in those days. I remember her saying to me once, "today I am making lamb stew, but without the lamb." Whatever it was she made, it was wonderful; and it was very important to her that there was always food around to serve. No one stopped by without getting a taste of something fantastic.

And the sweets! Ah, she knew how to please the grandchildren with sweets. I remember begging her for her zabaglione, which is a rich custard sweetened with wine. (Yes, wine! But a tiny amount . . .) Grabbing onto the apron, I would cry, "Please, Grandma, make me a zabaglione." And if I was extra good, she would. Even when she was eighty and could no longer cook, she would carry around her big black purse that always had a few candies rattling around the bottom for us kids.

These days, some people might say that was a form of emotional bribery, offering sweets for good behavior. You know what? That zabaglione was the best bribe I ever had.

It was important to her to solve problems. I remember once as a young girl complaining because I would always wear out my new pants because my inner thighs rubbed together (even then, I had these thighs to deal with!). One day I came home from school and she had sewn pieces of leather into the crotch and inner thighs of all my pants. I looked like the lone ranger in those pants! I was embarrassed to wear them in school, but to grandma Francesca's mind, she solved the problem.

She worked hard, and she played safe. She was always thinking of the future, and what the family needed. She micromanaged the household finances, and made do with what she had. She did her best to stretch the money, but would never think of taking advantage of someone else, or of taking what she considered a handout. She was much too proud for that.

Nothing was more important to her than her family. She would hound and hound people to make sure that they kept the family ties close. "Call your brother! It doesn't matter that he did something stupid. Call him!" The family would gather in her house at every holiday, and several times in between, not just for "special" occasions, but really the opposite: for ordinary occasions. Being with the family was the norm, not the exception. We didn't have to schedule "quality time."

She had common sense.

❧

In the coming chapters, I'm going to point out the things about modern life that are absurd—

> THE TRICK IS TO LISTEN TO YOUR "INNER GRANDMOTHER." SHE'S GOT A LITTLE MORE WISDOM THAN YOUR INNER CHILD.

the things that would have made Francesca look around and say **stunata!** You can try to hear the voice of your own grandparent, if you had one whom you consider wise. Or else think about an aunt, a godparent, someone from an earlier generation whose common sense you admire. The point is to keep conscious of how the earlier generation, the one that existed before the incessant pressure of media and marketing, managed to live their lives in such a way that they had less stress and anxiety and pain than we have today.

Of course, this is just a tool. In all cases, what you need to be doing is developing your own common sense. We are all filled with it, and deep down, we all know what's right, and what we need from our lives. We just get so bamboozled by the world around us that we have come to accept the ridiculous as the commonplace.

Listen to your inner voice, and you'll know what we all long for. We long for a world in which real human interaction is honored over virtual communication; where creativity and accomplishment is valued more in the workplace than doublespeak and exploitation; where civility is more important than faux spirituality; where health is more important than glamour; where we buy products for enjoyment, not out of intimidation; and where closeness is more cherished than status.

Those of you reading this who know my work know that I believe that laughter is the best medicine for our stressful times. Once we learn to lighten up and not take the small things so seriously, we find an enormous weight lifted off our shoulders. In this book, I want us all to laugh a lot at what a mess we've made of our daily lives. And through laughter, I want to help us separate the noise around us from the clarity within us. I want to help us stop bringing external pressures inside our bodies. I want us to stop blaming ourselves for not being the ideal specimen that the marketers put forth as normal.

I want to help us hear the voices of our grandmothers who would listen to some of the stuff we obsess about today, shake their heads in dismay, whack us on the side of the head and say: ***Just Stop It!***

And, in a nutshell, I want to help us get a grip on reality (as Robin Williams used to say, what a concept!) to help us remember the things that are important, which all too often get lost in the noise of modern life. We need to focus on the values that make human beings great: optimism, resiliency, hope, love, originality, good parenting, civility, altruism and moderation. The goal, for all of us, is to get back to a life that has less stress and more meaning, and I hope that laughing about the everyday insanity I talk about in this book can help you in the same ways that it helps me and the people I work with stay focused on the things that really matter.

Listen, every human being walking on earth has two things in common. We're all alive, and we're all going to end up dead. We can either let the absurdity of modern life drive us to the grave sooner, or we can laugh at it and have more fun while we're here. As I've said in my presentations and now in the title of this book, life is not a "stress" rehearsal. This is our one chance to live it in a way that is fun, that is filled with the wonders of love and human greatness, and that has meaning. In fact, instead of wasting our lives in a stress rehearsal, I want us to engage in *stress reversal!* Let's have less insanity and more fun.

Isn't that what it's all about?

1

Edgar Allan Poe
and Cousin Ignatz

*On individuality and our culture
of self-improvement*

I TOOK A TRIP RECENTLY to Los Angeles to give a corporate presentation, and the company I was speaking to put me up in one of the hip, trendy hotels in town. It's one of those places that is *so* hot, there's not even a sign outside to identify it. So if you're driving along Sunset Boulevard looking for it, you'd better know where you're going before you get there. I guess the idea is that if you're cool enough to stay there, you'll know where it is, and if not, it's the Days Inn for you. How's that for a warm welcoming attitude to start things off right?

Despite that, it's actually quite a nice hotel and has a fantastic restaurant and the staff found me pretty funny and entertaining to have around. They all walked around acting as if they barely noticed when a Sophia Loren clone checked in—but I could tell that it was all an act. The staff's disaffected and elitist attitude was part of what the hotel was selling. But I wouldn't buy it. I tried desperately to make them see the scene as I did: as a Fellini rerun. I'd make funny bored faces at them and grab my head with mock dismay and say things like, "Oh, God, no! Not another sunny day," or look disdainfully at a magnificent plate of *calamari fritti* and say, "How dull to have to eat like this day in and day out."

I think another reason they liked me is that just about every other guest I saw come and go in the lobby of that hotel looked and acted exactly the same. It was a little scary, as if I was watching a year 2000 version of *The Stepford Wives*. Everyone wore black t-shirts with black-framed narrow sunglasses and a white linen jacket and talked into a cell phone and carried a black leather shoulder bag out of which popped a bottle of mineral water. They all looked and acted as if this was the most boring place they'd ever been, and that they were totally unimpressed with the surroundings and the other people. Not a single eye looked around the room as if it were interested in what might be there, not a single voice said nice things to the staff, like "we're glad to be here!" Or "what a nice place you have here!" No, everyone was disinterested in everyone else and made it clear that they were so jaded that being in this lovely hotel meant nothing to them.

I guess being bored to tears has become a status symbol.

For me, the whole experience was stifling! The vitality, the energy, the joy, was totally missing. I was surrounded by people whose body language and temperament were like zombies, and the way they dressed was so incredibly dull that they might as well have been wearing a school uniform from 1957. No one looked eccentric, unusual, or interesting. Rather than standing out as individuals, they disappeared as if part of a huge ant farm.

This phenomenon worries me, and I think it's something that can be seen across our entire culture. We're becoming a very bland, vanilla society in which "fitting in" is critically important to people.

It makes sense, of course, given the mass media and constant marketing that is now such an inherent part of our society. After all, we are all constantly presented with the same models of perfection. We all look at photos of the same beautiful people in magazines, we all watch the same talking heads on television, we all go to see movies starring the same movie stars with the same disaffected personas. We all shop in malls that are so cookie-cutter that we can't tell if we're in our own town or in Outer Mongolia. We all listen to the same talk-show hosts and the same radio shows, so we're all constantly being given the same advice.

So before you know it, everybody wants the same clothes and strives to look like a model for J. Crew or Banana Republic or the Gap. Everybody goes to the same exercise classes fighting for the same body fat percentage. Everybody wants the same haircut and the same bone structure and the same nose. Everybody strives to have the same psychologically even temperament and the same balance of aggressiveness, empathy, cynicism and responsibility.

Social critic Bill McKibben states that "Boomers are the first generation born into the TV world—and thus conceived in the full-blown consumer society that has gotten more intense with every year. They're the first generation, for instance, to have watched something like 400,000 television commercials before age 20." What this leads to is a world in which we all are trying to fit a very narrow model of what's deemed by the media as acceptable in our society. And what's "in" is someone who is fit with washboard abs, who is well groomed, who wears clothes that look like they come from a chain store with wood paneling (or who may have a tattoo and a pierced navel to be edgy and hip, which is also "in"), who earns a respectable amount of money, who lives in a home in an upscale neighborhood, who has an even temper, who isn't in any way depressed or obsessive or manic or eccentric, who drives the proper car (or sport-utility vehicle) and who smells like something from the Body Shop.

Anybody who doesn't fit within maybe a narrow 10% range of what the society considers "normal" today is seen as some sort of deviant.

Do you doubt that we're pressured to "fit in?" Think for a minute about the massive industry today devoted to "self help."

There seems to be no limit to the stuff that people will write books about. Something like three thousand new self-help books get published every year. *Who would have guessed that we could have so many things wrong with us?* The subjects just get more and more narrow: books for adults with depression. Books for women on running with the wolves. Books for people with borderline personality disorder. I really saw a book the other day that promised to cure people of attention deficit disorder. Excuse me, but how are you going to get someone who has attention deficit disorder to SIT STILL LONG ENOUGH TO READ A BOOK?

The issue for me is this: these books, and the other media that produce endless self-help material—the magazines and talk shows and websites and newspaper columns—all contribute to a world in which we are constantly assaulted with the message that we have to fit a perfect mold, or else we're screwed up. How could people *not* feel this way? These days, if you read a magazine or watch television or look at bookstore shelves or read the newspapers, you can be damn sure you'll find some malady being discussed that will sound a little bit like something that affects you.

Did you have a second piece of toast with breakfast today? You can be sure that there's a radio talk show that will make you wonder if maybe you have an eating disorder. Have you been a little moody, or could you possibly have that bipolar disorder you read about in the *Times*? Did you stay up late last night surfing interesting sites on the Internet? Was it because you were engaged and excited and having fun, or is it that you're in danger of becoming a cyberaddict like that woman on the *Today* show?

And, likewise, as you peruse the media chances are (unless you're very lucky) that virtually no one you see in the pages of magazines or on television *looks* like you. They're all perfectly chiseled and fit and have big bright eyes and perfectly formed white teeth and asses the size of two ripe little peaches.

All of this contributes to a society in which, every minute of the day, we all walk around feeling as if we're just not good enough. And the first thing to go is our individuality.

Our society is so over-analyzed that every single thing we do—including the elements of our personalities that make us interesting, complex, complete human beings—has become fodder for self-help journalism and a reason for us to feel self-conscious and imperfect.

If you allowed it, the self-help media and marketers would convince you that just about every aspect of your physical and psychological self could be improved if you only worked at it. Didn't you know? There's not a thing about you that is fine just the way it is, from your temperament to your hair color to the sound of your voice to the size of your external organs. If you just read another book, or bought another product, or consulted with another expert, you could be just that one step closer to being a perfect human specimen. People are actually having elective surgery to change the shape of their sexual organs: a little bigger here, a little tighter there. Imagine! Taking a knife to that thing by choice. If that's not insane, what is?

Listen, it's exciting to engage in the process of self-discovery and self-improvement. But I worry that we've taken the journey to a place of self-obsession, where our attempts to *evolve* have made us *dissolve* into people who can never be at peace with ourselves.

How can we feel good about ourselves when a walk through the bookstore insists we:

Have thin thighs in thirty days.
Cure yourself of your toxic upbringing.
Attain the habits of highly successful people.
Awaken the giant within.
Make the most of your money.
Eat to win.
Heal your inner child.
Overcome overeating.
Take control of panic attacks.
Think like Leonardo da Vinci.
Learn Optimism.
Make your dreams come true.
Argue and win every time.
Have the courage to be rich.
Develop a superpower memory.
Improve your sense of direction and never get lost again!
Tap the wisdom and power of your heart's energy.
Find self-esteem in ten days.
Simplify your life.
Win the war within yourself.
Improve your emotional intelligence.
Dress for success.
Excavate your authentic self.
Discover the art of doing nothing.
Avoid the ten stupid things women do to mess up their lives.

I look at all those books and want to jump out the window. Who the hell could possibly live up to the demands of that self-help shelf? Because the subtext of each and every one of the titles of those books is: *you probably need this, don't you?*

> **You** *don't dress for success.*
> *You're* **NOT** *emotionally intelligent.*
> *You, over there, face facts. You eat to* **lose!**
> **Your** *inner child is writhing around in pain.*
> You, **yes you!** Stop sweating the small stuff!
> *You actually* **do** *the ten stupid things women do to mess up their lives,* **don't you? Admit it!!**

If you ask me, one of the silliest things someone could do to mess up their life is to pursue everything they read in self-help books.

Now, believe me, I'm far from the sort of person who thinks you shouldn't try to improve yourself. As you'll find out if you continue to read this book, my life has been a constant struggle for self-improvement, and I work very hard to help other people find ways to live richer, saner lives. My house is filled with self-help books.

But working toward improving yourself is a far cry from trying to make yourself perfect, and also a far cry from becoming a self-help junkie, which are the two trends I see over and over again among people.

A real problem for people in recent years is that marketers and the media have contributed toward making us a society in which we're all constantly faced with an impossibly high standard for self-improvement, all the time, in every area of our lives. No matter where we turn, we're faced with what amounts to a demand for how we could be improving ourselves; and of course that gives rise to a hidden accusation over everything that we have not yet fixed. Ultimately, if you pay attention, that can only lead to two possible results. You either become perfect, or you become angry and disappointed in yourself because you're not perfect.

It wasn't like this in our grandparent's day.

In previous generations, there was less obsession with being "the most that we can be." We didn't all have to have washboard abs, and if we had some obscure psychological quirk, we didn't know about it. And most importantly, nobody cared. We didn't know we had an inner child, so we didn't worry ourselves about how happy it was (in fact, if you ask me, maybe the inner child is so miserable because the outer grownup isn't having any fun!)

Every single move you make today can be interpreted as a symptom. Do you love your husband, or are you codependent? Do you enjoy sweets, or do you have an eating disorder? Are you horny or do you suffer from hypersexuality? Would you like to lose a pound or two, or do you have Body Dysmorphic Disorder?

Could you imagine Francesca worrying about this stuff? "Ah," she'd say, "I put on a pound or two. A little less pasta today." Or "I'm not feeling good today. Time to pray to Baby Jesus." She would not call Dr. Laura.

We're obsessed with finding out and fixing what's wrong with us, instead of enhancing and celebrating what's RIGHT with us.

I don't know about you, but I think that the drive we all have to fix all the things that are "wrong" with us is making the world an awfully boring place. And think of all the greatness that would be lost! You know what? If Edgar Allan Poe were alive today, he'd probably be taking an anger management program and we'd never have "The Cask of Amontillado" or "The Raven." Van Gogh would probably be a guest on Sally Jessy Raphael, and she'd try to get him back together with the woman for whom he cut off his ear! What a lesser world it would be if Rembrandt, Picasso, Dali, Michaelangelo, and Emily Dickenson had spent their lives learning self-empowerment rituals instead of practicing their art and feeling their pain.

What a wonderful place we'll be at if our culture could stop obsessing over what we do wrong, and ways in which we don't fit the mold, and instead really focus on the things that bring joy into our lives—laughter, connection, play, meaningful work—and our own creative individuality.

Instead of trying to persuade us to fit in, wouldn't it be nice if we lived in a society that encouraged uniqueness?

Remember how when we were teenagers the most important thing was to try to appear unique? We all tried so hard to stand out from the pack, to get ourselves noticed. It's something that seems to be genetic, that comes out of a genuine human need to display creativity and uniqueness. Even when teenagers take part in what seems to be a trend (witness today's wildly-colored hair dyes), they put their own spin on it.

Isn't it sad that that impulse to be unique somehow gets lost, and we all try to learn instead to fit in? Wouldn't it be wonderful to honor both human impulses? In the best of all psychological worlds, we would find a way to allow ourselves to be and feel unique while not doing things that are so bizarre that they intimidate others.

For me personally, I try to spend as much of my life as I can with "characters." You know, the people who really stand out from the crowd, who see things differently, who dare to look and act different, who behave eccentrically. I'm drawn to people who not only break the mold, they pulverize it into tiny pieces.

Maybe this started for me when I was a kid. At a very young age, I'd be sitting at a table in the kitchen in my parents' house, and I'd watch this strange group of characters parading in and out all the time. It was a circus:

There was a priest who would come by with relics that were blessed by another priest who, it was said, had a stigmata: the mark of the crucifixion. We never saw it, of course, but everyone believed it! My grandmother would carry around a vial filled with little bones that he would bring her, and all the adults would sit around with that priest in the kitchen and drink wine and tell stories. He was like our own Father Guido Sarducci!

There was a man who lived across the street from us, who had been a sailor. He was Sicilian, but he had a limey accent—I never understood why. He had a parrot that talked, and he had two daughters, and until he moved in across the street he had always lived in a houseboat. This was his first time on dry land, but I think maybe he still bobbed around a bit from the waves. One of his daughters, Peppi, who was about sixteen years old, used to take me to dance lessons. One night, I found her and my mother dancing around the living room floor with soapy brushes strapped to their feet, cleaning the lineoleum floor, singing arias from *The Barber of Seville*.

Peppi went on to be a professional Flamenco dancer.

Then there was Mrs. Burke, who lived on the third floor of our house. She was a nurse, and she'd come and go every day and the only thing she ever had to report about her work was that, "well, the patient died." I swear! It seemed like every other day she'd tell us about another patient who died. I don't know if she was slipping something into the IV's, but to me it seemed like she was Hannibal Lecter.

Down in the basement, my grandfather was making wine in a little still. He'd get raisins and rice, and make a wine that tasted like sake, and I'd go down there and be terrified by not only the sound of the fermenting (a glug-glug sound like someone slowly drowning—imagine what that did to the imagination of a six year old!), but also by this strange old model of a human skeleton he kept hanging in the basement.

And, believe it or not, there were live chickens running around down there. Don't ask me why. I'm not sure how they got there and I don't think we ever ate them. This was Brooklyn, not a farm for God's sake! I think my grand-father could have been arrested for having those chickens down there.

It was nutty. But my life was full of characters. I remember my old Great Aunt Ignatz, who was really my grandmother's first cousin. *Ignatzia* we'd call her in Italian. Wandering around late at night, she'd talk to herself. She wasn't crazy, but she sure was a little weird. She didn't pay attention, and she was a little hard of hearing.

We lived in a neighborhood not far from the shoreline, and we'd hear the foghorns from the ships out in the bay. Whenever Ignatzia would hear a foghorn, she'd turn to my grandmother and ask "Whatsa matta, Francesca? Your stomach is bothering you?" The kids would run out of the room and squeal with laughter.

Then there was her daughter, Fran, whose house we used to go visit. Or, maybe I should say, whose museum we'd visit. You'd go visit this woman's home, and she'd take you for a tour of the upstairs that was beautifully decorated and spotless. You'd have to walk around the whole place— "here's the kitchen, here's the living room, here's the bathroom." It was lovely. It looked like no one lived there.

And guess what? *No one did.* You'd get to look around at the upstairs, but God forbid you should touch anything. Then she'd lead you back down to the basement to another whole house, and that's where you were allowed to hang around. The upstairs was there just to show you what good taste she had.

Now, here's my point. Yes, cousin Ignatz and Fran were

> PEOPLE WHO DON'T FEEL
> PRESSURE TO CONFORM TO
> SOCIETAL STANDARDS LIVE
> LONGER, HAPPIER LIVES.

a little nuts. But they were interesting. Having them around made life in the family more fun and more stimulating. We'd laugh every time we went to their houses. They were unique, they were charming, having them around generated tons of laughter.

And it was an innocent laughter. We weren't making fun of them, they were family! We appreciated them as characters and as people we loved, and we appreciated the fact that they were eccentric as hell.

You know that today, Ignatz would be on Prozac and Fran would be in analysis—and they'd both be wearing clothes from Banana Republic and taking Spinning classes at the gym.

We seem to no longer be able to truly appreciate the unusual in people, and I think that's sad for all of us. Quirky people bring richness to the world, they help forge new territory, they see things the rest of us don't see. But many of us are put off by them, we've been trained to think that if people are a little unusual, if they don't fit the mold, that they're a little scary. We act as if their eccentricity is a fatal flaw, and we avoid them the way we too often avoid the sick or the poor. For many eccentrics, it's not a flaw. In fact, it's the exact opposite.

David Weeks of England performed a major study of

eccentrics, and discovered that they actually live longer, happier lives. His study revealed that because they don't feel the need to conform to societal norms, they live with a more optimistic outlook, and less stress, than the rest of us.

The Tombstone No One Wants #1

HERE LIES JANE DOE.

SHE WAS PRETTY MUCH

LIKE EVERYBODY ELSE.

Isn't this another big "duh"? It proves that those of us who don't feel pressure to fit in are happier. And for the rest of us, therefore, it makes sense to conclude that the more we try to fit in, the more miserable we're becoming.

The human animal is designed so that we're all different, both physically and psychologically. Some of us will be born with genes that make us muscular, some with genes that make us skinny, some with genes that make us fat. Some of us are born with genes that make us naturally calm, some naturally tense, some naturally angry. The human experience is one of diversity, and while we pay a lot of lip service these days to wanting diversity in our society, we all know that in fact, even those of us of different races and heritages are becoming more homogeneous.

Why is it that an inordinate number of women today have self-image problems? Think about it: how awful to be a woman today, in a culture in which fitting a certain body image is so profoundly important to people? How awful for the majority of women (and men too) to never feel comfortable in their own bodies, because their bodies don't fit some ideal standard that has been marketed to us as what we should aspire to.

My grandmother was a square, stout little woman. She wasn't obese, she wasn't even really fat. But she was soft. Every now and then she might have gotten on the scale and she'd say "Ahh! How'd those five pounds get there?" But that didn't change the way she felt about herself. She kept going, and she made her macaroni, and stuffed her peas, or whatever the hell else she was doing. Maybe she'd eat a little less to make up for those five pounds. But she felt good about who she was and her place in the world. Five extra pounds on the scale was not a life or death issue.

It's hard to believe, but people then were so different. The world was different. Their lives were smaller. There was no television, most people didn't read glossy magazines, they went to the movies now and then, and the people in the movies were presented as ideals, not as real people they could ever actually aspire to look like. They were surrounded by their own small world of friends and family, and that was the only community they needed to feel a part of.

They were not barraged with information that told them ways that they needed to change themselves and help themselves and make their lives better. They weren't assaulted with marketing

> LET'S FACE IT, TRYING TO BE "THE BEST THAT YOU CAN BE" IS EXHAUSTING!

techniques that made them feel deformed for having a little cellulite, or like they should go check into the mental ward because they felt like having fried eggs for breakfast.

Now we are given the hard-core facts behind everything. We know exactly what our body-fat ratio ought to be, we know what disorders we are prone to, we know what clothes we should be wearing, and we're obsessed with "being the best that we can be." Virtually every message sent to us by the media and by the marketing of almost every product for sale in America is that "you can improve yourself." And ultimately, for millions of people, our obsession with improving ourselves is killing us.

Many people, in their quest for self-improvement, have become so dreadfully serious and stressed out and *dull* that they're losing what's most important about life. Fun! Connection! Pleasure! Excitement! How many times have you heard people go on and on about what they ate today? The fat police: "I ate a slice of pizza at lunch, I just can't believe it! I'm going to have to work out twice as hard tonight!" Don't you just want to say "SHUT THE HELL UP! This is BORING! Why the hell should I care about what YOU eat?"

Don't you ever want to just yell "I ate like a PIG today! And I loved every minute of it!"

How shocking would THAT be in today's society? I know people who would commit suicide before saying such a thing. And what is it, really? What's so terrible? It's simply admitting that you enjoy a pleasure that nature gave you.

But to admit that you enjoy eating means admitting

you're not a superior being. Superior beings survive on two carrot sticks, a square of tofu and a power bar.

So many people come up to me at my seminars and tell me what's wrong with them. Just a few weeks ago a woman who sat quietly through a day-long presentation—who participated but without a lot of gusto—came up to me afterward and told me that she thought her life had changed that day. She was so moved by the things I was saying that she was going to make big changes in her life.

I couldn't help but say to her, "It's funny, I wouldn't have guessed that you were so affected by this. You didn't participate much, you didn't laugh very much. It seemed like you were just sitting through it."

She lowered her voice to a whisper, and went on to tell me that she felt very self-conscious over that fact that her teeth are a little misshapen. She's in the process of having dental work done, but she feels just too awkward to laugh or to smile.

What a horrible pressure for a human being to have to live with! To not laugh because it would show an imperfection.

Everyone has faults, everyone has neuroses, everyone has physical imperfections, and everyone has psychological quirks. The ones that you have are the things that make you unique. Don't only live with them, enjoy them and make the most of them (In fact, have you noticed that very recently the top models all seem to have some imperfection that makes them interesting?)! Flaunt them!

If you want to change, of course, work toward changing the things you want to change. Keep in mind, however, that changing behaviors involves complex interactions between genes, brain chemistry and lifestyle. Self-improvement is a never-ending quest that should be part of everyone's life, all the time. But make sure it's on your own terms. Of course the woman in my seminar should have orthodontia work done to improve her smile, if that's what's important to her, but why couldn't she also laugh freely and enjoy life in the interval?

You have to use your intuition, your common sense, your intelligence and your own idiosyncratic sense of right and wrong to tell you what things about you need changing. Since we live in a world where self-help advice is presented to us everywhere we turn, we need to think long and hard about which pieces of self-help advice are helpful and which are ridiculous.

You have to look toward your own common sense—and ask your inner grandmother—when dealing with self-help gurus. Think long and hard: *does this piece of advice feel right and will it improve my life, or does it feel wrong and does it have the* potential *to make me feel more stressed and more inadequate?* You must remain authentic to yourself. Don't become the advice. When we give up ourselves to become like other people, we end up disliking not only that other person, but ourselves as well. Engage in learning, but don't disengage from your own beliefs.

I read a parenting book recently that recommended letting a child sleep in the parents' bed as long as the child likes, even through age five or six. That is the way primitive cultures raised their children, and this particular author believed that it was in the best interest of kids to allow this to go on.

Well, yeah. But primitive cultures went to the bathroom in their backyards, too. That doesn't make it right for most people today. For many people I know, such advice would ruin their lives. When both parents are getting up at 7 A.M. to go to the office and getting home at six to cook dinner and have a little conversation, how are you going to survive with a five-year-old sleeping in the middle, kicking you all night long?

You've got to choose what feels right for you. I can't say that letting a kid sleep in the parental bed until puberty isn't right for some families. I'm sure it can be lovely. But if it's NOT right for you, don't saddle yourself with guilt because someone else believes you're doing something wrong. Take that book, throw it out the window, and move on.

Remember that people who write self-help books, or who have TV talk shows or write for magazines, don't know everything about everybody (some don't seem to know anything about anybody!). Remember that what they're saying may be right for some people some time, but only you know what's right for you.

We've got to honor the things about us that are individual, the things that separate us, the things that make us stand out in the crowd. These are the things that make us human, and that make us the artists of our own canvas.

All the little details of your life are the things that give your canvas the color; they are your palette, if you will. And the people that we remember, the people who are full of life and energy and who infuse others with their power, are the ones whose palettes are the most colorful.

In fact, it is the people who paint totally outside the lines whom we remember most vividly. And don't forget that every canvas has shades of light and of darkness. Don't be afraid to sometimes look at the negative. We learn from the entire palette.

If you want to add more color, energy and fun to your life, surround yourself with people who break the mold. They are easy to spot. Look for the person at a party who is dressed flamboyantly, creating the phenomenon rather than becoming part of one. Next time you go out shopping, don't go to the Gap, go to some funky shop that sells antique clothes and costumes. You'll meet a lot more interesting people there.

The more you're surrounded by people who break the mold, the more you'll feel comfortable in doing it yourself. And it is so important for each of us to do whatever we can to overcome our desire to fit in.

Be bizarre! Act crazy, take chances, dare to be embarrassed. When I throw a party, I invite the most unusual people I can find. It drives my husband crazy, but I have a blast!

What we need to do

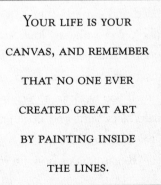

YOUR LIFE IS YOUR CANVAS, AND REMEMBER THAT NO ONE EVER CREATED GREAT ART BY PAINTING INSIDE THE LINES.

as individuals is try to step out of the box that everyone else is trying to fit into. And it doesn't have to be extreme. You don't need to walk down the street dressed like a giant peacock with your collection of trolls. You need to tap into your inner artist and create your own masterpiece.

Think about nature, and the way that flowers bloom in the wild. There's nothing orderly about it, the colors grow everywhere, the shapes go wild. Nothing is ever out-of-place. The reds look wonderful next to the purples next to the yellows and next to the greens. The tall-blooming roses look fantastic surrounded by the low yellow daisies.

You can do anything and look like anything! Make a statement, and it doesn't have to be big. Wear a pair of funky sunglasses or an elaborate piece of jewelry. Wear a wild tie. Splash yourself with color.

If you're too self-conscious to allow yourself to stand out in big ways, start in very small ways. How about a briefcase that's an unusual shape? How about sexy underwear beneath that gray suit? A flower in your lapel? In your hair?

When everyone else is acting like they're bored and jaded and can't bother to take notice of a beautiful hotel lobby, you walk in, look around, throw your bags to the ground and yell "WHOOPEE!!! I have never, ever seen anything so beautiful in my entire life!"

If you work in an environment where everyone wears little black suits and little gray silk blouses, wear BRIGHT RED POLKADOTS!

Regardless of how fit you may be, look in the mirror

(naked, if you dare) and say "Aren't I AMAZING? I'M ALIVE! And everything works!"

Laugh at self-help articles. Read them aloud, with as much dramatic flair as possible, to your families. Act as if you were reading Shakespeare: "To have thin thighs, or not to have thin thighs? Who the hell cares?"

Think of the little ways you exhibited your individuality in childhood. Did you dress up? Wear hats? Wear costumes? Act out plays? Did you run? Jump? Skip?

Do what you can to bring those little pleasures into your everyday life and use them to enrich your canvas. Children never paint inside the lines, and they're so much freer for it.

⤜∾⤐

Throughout this book, I'm going to end every chapter with a selection of ten questions. These questions are meant to make you think (and, sometimes, make you laugh . . .) about the issue discussed in the chapter. Since our inner wisdom sometimes likes to be elusive—or is itself confused from being constantly hammered by media images—you need to be vigilant about asking yourself questions, over and over. We can not always trust that what we hear in our heads is our own inner voice. We could be listening to a voice planted there, or influenced, by constant media exposure.

One of the great philosophers of all time, Socrates, believed that we possess inside of us all the knowledge we need, but that the answers are often hard for us to see. He be-lieved that the only way to unlock our internal knowledge is to constantly ask questions, questions that look at the same issue from several angles and several different points of view, until one is able to draw one's own conclusions.

This philosophy of relentless questioning is still called the Socratic method.

It seems to me that when we try to separate reality from absurdity, only this sort of self-questioning will help us to avoid the trap of simply going along with the common societal trends. So I'm going to play Socrates: think of me in a Toga and ignore the thighs that rub together. But re-member, the thing about Socrates and Socratic thinking is that you couldn't ask the teacher a question; the teacher asked the student. Unlike most other books out there that tell you what you should be thinking, this one is simply go-ing to ask you the questions you should ask yourself.

The brilliant writer, philosopher and activist Elie Weisel was recently quoted as saying "I teach my students how to ask questions. In the word 'question' there is a beau-tiful word—quest . . . the essential questions have no an-swers."

Think of your wise grandmother or grandmother-sub-stitute as the person looking over your shoulder as you stop and ask yourself these questions. Then, think long and hard about the meaning of your answers. Don't rush this. Take at least five minutes with every question. The insights may surprise you.

If you want to really increase the intimacy and the

level of understanding this process will bring to your life, discuss these questions with someone you trust. Elie Weisel also said "The moment we have answers, there is no dialogue. Questions unite people; answers divide them. So why have answers when you can live without them?"

Take a Socrates Break.
Don't ask me, ask yourself:

❖ *Do you ever act bored or jaded to cover up the fact that you're embarrassed to show how excited you really are?*

❖ *Do you browse the self-help section of bookstores and let the selection there guide you into thinking of things that need improvement?*

❖ *Have you ever followed advice in a self-help book or article, even though that advice seemed a little strange to you, assuming the "expert" knew better?*

❖ *Do eccentric people scare you, or interest you?*

❖ *When you buy clothing, how important is it to you that the clothes look like what other people in your circle wear?*

❖ *How does it make you feel when you break a pattern? Take a different route to work? Try a new cuisine?*

❖ *How many of your friends have lifestyles that are quite different from yours (are of a different race, sexual orientation, social standing)?*

❖ What was it that made you "stand out" in high school? How long has it been since you've done whatever that was?

❖ Is there something about you that you try to hide because it's not like everybody else?

❖ What exactly would happen to you if you exposed that hidden thing?

2

All Work and No Play

On sanity and the workplace

ONE OF THE WORST EXPERIENCES of my work life happened almost thirty-five years ago, and it's an episode I fondly refer to as the "dog crap story."

At the time, I was a young divorced mother, raising three kids on my own with almost no money in the bank, and I was really struggling, day-to-day, to pay our bills and keep food on the table. My ex-husband was responsible about child support payments, but still, there never seemed to be enough.

After being married for sixteen years, or being a "geisha," as I like to say, I was stuck between a rock and a hard place. I had no real marketable skills. I had spent a lot of my free time during my married years working on my career as an artist, and I actually sold a few paintings during those tough first years on my own, but I sure wasn't going to earn a living that way. I had a B.A. in speech therapy. That didn't have people banging down my doors throwing money at me for my brilliant business insights. And I had three kids to feed and clothe and keep in warm beds. It wasn't easy, to put it mildly.

I literally had to sell wedding gifts to pay the bills. I once sold a twelve-piece setting of sterling silver for $150. I sold furniture. I was doing whatever work I could find. I waited tables at Friendly's for a short while. I hung wallpaper. At one point I found myself cooking meals at a local tennis club, and I used that experience as an opening to start making some regular money doing catering of gourmet meals.

I went back to school and started studying for a masters in dance therapy—and that's when I got the idea that it might be fun to mix music with exercise. This was long before it was common practice—Jackie Sorenson, who created Jazzercise, the predecessor to aerobics, hadn't even started doing it yet—but I convinced a local health spa chain to hire me to develop a program for them.

Believe it or not, everyone was skeptical of this idea, as if we were talking about putting customers on rockets and sending them to the moon. Before my daring employers sent me out on the road to start teaching my program to the trainers at the individual clubs, my bosses would warn me, in the most serious and dour tones they could muster up, *be careful, be careful. Don't go too fast. People will be scared of this.*

Can you believe how stupid this was? Talk about a big "duh!" But my bosses were right in understanding how set in their ways were these trainers and club managers. I'd go around and have to show these people: "here's how the exercise class looks *without* music; and now here's what it looks like *with* music." *Here's something really dull and boring; here's something lively and exciting and fun.* But they just couldn't believe that the customers might actually like exercise classes with music. I got fought every step of the way and ultimately, I got fired for "not fitting in."

Funny, that's not the only time I've heard that.

But, guess what: people liked exercising with music. I was a little ahead of my time.

So I was off on my own again and had these three kids to support. But I really believed in what I was doing so I took my last paycheck, rented a small local Elks hall, and sent out invitations to everybody I knew to come take my exercise class with music. Seventy-five people signed up for that first class.

And that's really what started my career as an entrepreneur. I started renting halls one event at a time, and letting my core group of clients know where and when I'd run a class—and people would come. And I went gangbusters at it and worked all the time and soon I was able to have a friend, Beverly, who was also a divorced single mother, work with me. Before long we incorporated wellness issues into the program I was teaching, and things were starting to look up.

I still had no money, but at least I didn't have to sell off my belongings any longer to feed the kids.

Beverly and I were working our butts off. We'd rent a hall, we'd advertise, we'd bring in refreshments, we'd run a class. We'd start all over again. We'd travel all over the region, but never so far that we couldn't get home to our kids at night. It was crazy, but we made it work.

Then we met a woman who owned a beauty shop in Norwell, a nearby town. In the back of her shop she had another business: a dog kennel. She had decided to get rid of the kennel, which was housed in this rather large separate building. When we met this woman and she heard about our fledgling fitness business, she said "I've always wanted to have a spa."

That's how we began our conversations with her about taking that dog kennel and turning it into a spa. We had long meetings and brainstorming sessions. It was an idea that excited us enormously. We would create programs in exercise and wellness, combining that with more beauty and skin care offerings along with the services her beauty parlor was already offering. We'd have her clientele as a base of business.

She was going to finance this, since we didn't have any money. We would do our part by supplying all the labor and the marketing. This was in the middle of the winter, and the plan was to get the business up and running by spring. We had to turn the dog kennel into a studio and locker rooms.

Now picture this if you can: Beverly and I—two young divorced mothers—spent much of that winter bundled up in heavy coats, with huge pick-axes, chipping away at concrete and frozen dog shit.

Yes, that's right. Frozen dog shit. We spent months out in the bitter cold, walking back and forth from a little gas heater that kept us warm. We'd stand by the fire for a minute, and then go back and battle the poop. Once, while taking a moment off to thaw my feet, my boots caught fire.

In between our sessions with the pick-axes, we'd be hustling to sign up members for the spa.

Finally, after months and months of this, when things were shaping up and the weather was getting warmer and sheetrock walls were actually going up, just as Beverly and I were starting to actually feel like this dream was going to become a reality, we found out that our partner, the beauty-salon owner, had never applied for a permit. The building was zoned for dogs, not for people. The town wouldn't grant a variance.

We had to give money back to 150 people who had already signed up for annual memberships.

All that frozen dog shit, and nothing to show for it.

I tell this story for this reason: what I really remember from that time, despite all the hardship and the disappointment and the back-breaking work and the humiliation of that experience, was Beverly and I laughing our asses off.

The absurdity of us two young mothers out there in our winter coats and our heavy gloves with pick-axes in our hands and our boots catching fire was, you have to admit, hilarious. And we had a sense of humor about the situation and about ourselves.

We were out there chipping away at the crap, knowing that in two hours we had to get home and pick the kids up from school and cook dinner and get them to take baths and do homework and all the other impossible details of running a home. Yet, I remember that we laughed and laughed till we made ourselves sick.

We knew that we'd survive. That we'd move on, and that what we were going through was so absurd that we had to laugh about it.

It's a disturbing trend I see that today, many many people simply do not find the time to laugh, or to bring fun into their work lives. They take their jobs and their careers so seriously that they leave no room for humor or for lightness. "Me? Laugh? I'm much too busy to laugh; besides, this is serious business we do here. Very serious."

I walk around the offices of some of the companies I consult for, and I think I'm walking through a funeral parlor! You see it on the faces, the furrowed brows, the eyes darting back and forth, the suspicious glances when you walk down the hall. I always want to give my condolences.

These are supposed to be creative places. Why do they feel like morgues?

I think it's because the humor has been beaten out of us. We're afraid that if it looks like we're having fun, we won't be taken seriously enough. So we walk quickly around the workplace, we always look like we're very busy. Even when we're at our desk reading a memo, we do it very intently and intensely. We narrow our eyes and stare. We make it clear to anyone walking by that we're working. Yes, working. God forbid it should be a little fun.

And even more distressing is the fact that many of us have been forced to make our worklife our entire life. We live in a time in which technology has connected us to the workplace all the time, so we're never really away. And add on top of that a competitive corporate environment in which we are all meant to feel that there is someone

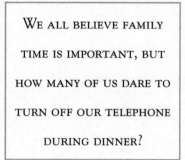

WE ALL BELIEVE FAMILY TIME IS IMPORTANT, BUT HOW MANY OF US DARE TO TURN OFF OUR TELEPHONE DURING DINNER?

else out there who will do our job for less money, and we're hit with the psychological double-whammy of feeling that we have a **responsibility** to get everything done; and a **paranoia** over what might happen to us if we don't.

The American employee now works more hours per year—two full weeks worth!—than any industrialized nation in the world, including Japan!

The additional working time has got to be taken away from somewhere, of course. And for most of us, the only place from which to steal the time is from time previously spent having a rich inner life and a rich family life.

And doesn't it make sense that in our current society, in which everyone works these insane hours, that we start to act as if workaholism is something admirable? It seems like every day I hear people talking about someone who works eighteen-hour days and travels to three cities a week and is in their office every Saturday and never sees their kids . . . And what is said about them? "Wow, aren't they something? They just don't stop! They're amazing." I want to say: "What the hell is wrong with them? Are they out of their minds?

> WE'RE ALWAYS TALKING ABOUT HOW HARD WE WORKED: *"I stayed in the office till ten last night,"* OR *"I've worked through two meals today."* AND WE SAY IT AS IF IT'S SOMETHING TO BE PROUD OF. WHY DON'T WE EVER COMPETE OVER HOW MUCH FUN WE HAD? HOW PLAYFUL WE'VE BEEN? HOW MUCH TIME WE SPENT WITH OUR FAMILIES? *"Oh yeah, John, you spent the day at the playground? Well, I was up until ten reading Harry Potter to my daughter."*

Don't they know that there's more to life than answering their e-mails? Have they thought about what they're going to miss once they're in their coffin?"

Think of our grandparents' generation: it was unheard of for them not to stop. You came home, you had dinner with your family, you read the paper, you read the kids a story. There was work time, and there was personal time. A firm line in the sand separated the two. Now there's no such thing as personal time.

My grandfather Lorenzo owned a little store in Brooklyn where he sold fresh breads and pasta, made there on the premises. It was incredibly hard work, and long hours. He was at the store before sunrise to start getting the breads ready, and he was there into the night, getting things ready for the next day. Saturday was a busy day.

But when he was home, he was home. I never had to worry about him pushing me off his lap to grab the cell phone. He wasn't powering up the laptop and checking inventory when it was time to put me to bed. When we had his attention, we had his full attention.

People don't even take lunch hours anymore. They see lunch hour as a way to "catch up" on work, so they sit there and answer e-mails or phone calls or write letters or read reports, and they grab a sandwich or something at their desks.

Have you ever watched someone eat lunch at their desk? It's an utterly unconscious act, they could be eating that frozen dog crap I dug up and never even know it. The food that they ingest may well take care of some nutritional needs, but what about the need to feel pleasure? To feel nurtured? To unwind and take a break?

That's gone.

And then there's the vacation. When our grandparents took a vaca-

> ### The Tombstone No One Wants #2
>
> HERE LIES JANE DOE.
>
> RETURNED EVERY E-MAIL.
>
> MET EVERY DEADLINE.
>
> MISSED TWELVE ELEMENTARY SCHOOL PERFORMANCES AND THIRTY-FIVE DINNER DATES WITH HUSBAND.

tion, they took a *vacation*! They went with their families someplace out of town, usually to the mountains where it was cooler, and they spent a week or more cut off from their normal day-to-day existence. It was a time to refresh their souls and nurture their connections to family.

But now? A friend of mine recently told me about what sounded like a lovely vacation he was planning to take with his wife and family to the coast of Maine. They were renting a house on a remote island where their children could play on the beach right outside the living room while the adults stayed on the deck and had cocktails. There was hiking nearby, the sound of lobster boats in the morning, and clam-digging right off their front porch. It sounded perfect, and particularly right for a couple trying to escape a high-pressure life in New York City.

He and his wife are both professionals, and they were going away for two weeks.

I think it took them two weeks to pack their office equipment.

They had to pack their fax machine, because, who knows? Somebody might have to send them an important document that they'd die without seeing before they returned. They each brought a laptop computer, of course, so that they could continue to have at their fingertips the same millions of bits of information that is available to them at their offices there on the beach with them on the coast of Maine. You never know, they might wake up in the middle of the night with a great idea and need the address of that person who they once met at a cocktail party three years ago, who is dutifully listed in their database.

I know that it took my friend several hours of head-scratching conversations with the tech guy at his company to figure out how to log on to the office computer so that he could download his e-mail. Then, once he arrived at the house in Maine, it took him several more hours to find a local Internet access service he could log on to.

They packed their home telephone answering machine, because, after all, the rental house might not have one, and suppose someone called while they went out for a walk? My God, that person might have to listen to an unanswered ring and try again later.

Of course, that assumes that the person who called didn't have the number for my friend's cell phone, which eagerly waited inside his backpack whenever the family went out for a hike in the woods.

Excuse me. Is this a vacation?

They didn't go on vacation. They just took their office with them as an additional guest. The office went on a vacation. The fax machine had a lovely time at the beach.

I asked him why he didn't just have a truck come and dump some sand on the floor in the middle of his office. He could buy one of those tapes with the sound of the waves crashing, and play it in the background. Wouldn't that have been easier?

This is total absurdity. But it's become very hard for us to see that reality. It's because our society fosters an illusion

> HOW MANY PEOPLE
> REALLY NEED PAGERS?
> IS SOMEONE GOING TO
> LIVE OR DIE IF THEY
> MISS A CALL, OR IS
> THAT VIBRATING
> THING A TURN-ON?

that unless you are in constant communication with the people you work with, you must not be very important. If you're not in touch, then things could happen without you. And once people realize that things could go on without you, how long until someone decides that they don't need you there at all? So we find ourselves searching, faxing, phoning, instant-messaging, voice-mailing and remaining in constant contact to feed into both our inherent sense of responsibility (yes, we try to get back to people as soon as possible) and our fear of being replaced.

Everyone believes that they can't get away, they can't take some time just for themselves and their families. Their bosses need them. Their staff needs them. Their clients need them. Their patients need them. Everybody needs them. But consider: if something really critical happened, if there was an accident and a child was hurt, say, then who would give a damn about their staff or their clients?

Eight years ago, when my husband had a heart attack, everything stopped. I was supposed to be the keynote speaker at the American Red Cross conference and guess what? I had to cancel on them. They weren't happy, but you know what? Nobody stopped breathing as a result of me not being the keynote speaker.

When you really need to, you *can* escape.

> PEOPLE SAY TO ME: "AS SOON AS I GET AHEAD OF MY WORK, I'LL TAKE SOME TIME OFF." "OH, AND WHAT WILL YOU DO WITH YOUR TIME OFF?" "CALL PEOPLE BACK."

How important is your life? How important are the moments you spend with your loved ones? You'd be out of touch with your office for several days if there was a medical emergency. Isn't spending uninterrupted time with the people you love just as important as that? In fact, isn't the lack of time you have for loved ones in itself an emergency?

I told my friend who took the trip to Maine: take at least two days. Just two days for God's sake. Put a message on the machine: "I'm spending time with my family. I'll get back to you on Thursday." If there's anyone in his life who would begrudge him those two days, that person shouldn't be in his life anyway.

I find it amazing that so many people just don't seem to realize that the cemetery is filled with people who took their fax machines to the beach. Now those people are missing a lot of faxes. E-mails, too.

But the phenomenon of people feeling constantly connected and wired to their jobs is just the beginning of what's wrong with today's workplace.

The modern workplace doesn't allow people to really be people. It often doesn't even honor the needs of the hu-

> OFFICE BUILDING MANAGERS SAY THAT THE REASON WINDOWS DON'T OPEN IS TO PROTECT PEOPLE FROM JUMPING OUT. *What?* HOW MANY PEOPLE DIED FROM THE PROBLEM OF OPEN WINDOWS IN OUR GRANDPARENTS' GENERATION? MAYBE THEY SHOULD LOOK AT WHAT'S GOING ON INSIDE THAT MAKES PEOPLE FEEL THAT THEY WANT TO JUMP OUT A WINDOW.

man body. It shoves us into little cubicles, makes us see with unnatural light, makes us breathe re-circulated air, and makes us pray for the day when we are important enough to the organization that we can have an office with a window.

Is that a big "duh" or what? To have to work in an environment that feels as inauthentic as the inside of the space shuttle when, nine times out of ten, it's in an office park in some suburb that could just as easily offer natural light and fresh air?

Whose idea was this?

When you stop and ask yourself questions like "whose idea was this?" and "why does it have to be this way?" you have to face the fact that, indeed, whoever did it (namely: your employer) is probably someone who doesn't really care all that much about the human spirit. Or, at least, that he cares more about bringing home big profits than he does about honoring the physical and emotional needs of the staff.

And, for those who work in big corporations, knowing that the CEO of the company has taken home sometimes tens of millions of dollars in salary and stock options, sitting in a little cubicle feels more and more insulting.

I was hired by a big company to do a motivational program for them, and it's a company that is in the business of often serving customers late into the night. So, the human resources person called me up and said he wanted to discuss the "issues" of their company with me. Now, I could have been really obnoxious and told him that he didn't have to bother. I know the issues, they're always the same. People are burning out; the stress level is high; there is a lot of anger and tension in the workplace. Many of their employees have a hard time dealing with responsibility. They have a high rate of turnover.

Of course, I didn't. I listened politely. Francesca would have wagged her finger at me from the great beyond if I had done otherwise.

But the thing that was a little different about this company was the work hours. The high-pressure time went much later into the night than many businesses; they served their customers well past midnight. So I asked him: Has your company looked into circadian rhythms and how that affects work and productivity?

Of course, he acted as if I was speaking a foreign language. This was just a little too weird.

I told him how scientific studies have now proven that the rhythms of the body, the "body clock" that is hard-wired into all of us, have profound effects on the way we perform. Scientists now think that the body reacts differently to drugs, to certain tests, and can even be more susceptible to certain diseases and symptoms **at different hours of the day**. Sleep deprivation in and of itself creates irritability, suppressed immune response, and, of course, drowsiness and carelessness.

Since a great deal of this company's particular business had to do with employees working long, late, and inconsistent hours, it seemed to me a natural thing for them to consider.

His response was a rote, "Well, I never thought of that. I guess we should look into it," but it was said with a tone that made it abundantly clear that he never would.

So, what this company really was saying to me was, **"come in, do your thing, rally the troops, get people excited,"** but they had no real interest in looking deeper to solve the problem. They didn't want to have to deal with whole people. They wanted to pump them up, give them awards and a big, lavish dinner at their annual conference. They wanted to have me make them laugh and forget their problems for a night.

But do they ever ac-

CAN ANYONE EXPLAIN TO ME THE APPEAL OF EVEN *thinking* OF WORKING "24/7"?

tually think: How many hours of sleep are these people getting? Do they get decent meals, and are they eating well? Are they exercising? How are they taking care of themselves?

The workplace today doesn't honor whole human beings—and that's a serious problem.

Now, I don't necessarily think that it's the role of a corporation to take care of people's souls. People do that for themselves. But in our grandparents' generation the companies didn't expect people to work around-the-clock (or, my favorite buzzword, **24/7**). In those days, even though the companies may not have honored the entire human being, at least they honored the fact that their employees had lives outside of the workplace. That difference gave the employees the time to honor themselves.

Let's Get Real

For so many people, the workplace has become more than just their job—more than the "daily grind"—it's become the way they define themselves and the way they feel important. They look to their careers as their key to status, self-importance, inner worth.

They get obsessed with their job title: as if becoming a "senior vice president" instead of a "vice president" really makes them someone different, or someone better. And the titles are so complicated that they don't really help enlighten anyone as to what someone does, or what their role is in the hierarchy of a company. What's the real point? Excuse me, but is the "executive vice president and managing director of corporate initiatives and planning" anybody's boss? And what the hell does he do?

I wish the corporate world used titles like the mafia. See him? He's the boss; that one, he's the underboss; the other one is a soldier. And that one over there? He's the boss of bosses. *Now* I understand what's what!

I walk around the offices of people I consult with and they show me the boss's office and say in whispered tones: "oh, of course he has this lovely corner office." As if that person has achieved something truly wonderful. Excuse me? He has a view of the outside world. Shouldn't everyone?

I find myself talking to people who take me aside and confide in me, telling me their stories. They think that their boss doesn't like them, they think they're going to be fired. They're distraught. Should they get a new job, should they simply stay quiet and hope things get better?

But the one thing almost no one tells me they're thinking of doing is the one thing I always think they *should* be doing (which maybe explains why I could never work in a corporate environment): I think they should be speaking their minds and uncovering the truth. I think they should be going up to the boss and saying "I don't think things feel right between us. Can we talk about this?"

The study of humanistic psychology would say that once you begin to divest yourself of bits of who you are, you become inauthentic—or you feel like a phony to yourself.

And that raises irritability and self-directed anger because you're pretending to be someone you're not.

And, sadly, it seems to me that the contemporary workplace has become a place where very few people feel that they can be authentic. The messages are often clearly sent: **we don't want to hear about your problems; we want to hear your ideas, but only if they agree with ours; we want you to be happy here, but if you're miserable that's your problem**. How could anyone feel comfortable, natural, and creative in that sort of an environment?

I have a friend who, a couple of years ago, took a job that was clearly wrong for him. He is a very talented guy, and when we first met he was at a company where he was honored and where he felt like he could be himself. He was open and fun to be around and creative and effective in his position.

Then he took a new job in a much bigger company and the next time I saw him, he was literally twitching. I couldn't believe it. I thought he would jump out of his seat! I sat in his office and I could tell that he was trying hard to concentrate on what I was saying, and to enjoy my company the way he used to, but his eyes kept wandering to the door. And he kept twitching.

Do buzzwords really help matters? Is it any better to be downsized or re-engineered than it is to be fired?

I realized that, psychologically, he was in a hypervigilant state, which is the state that cavemen would get into when they were wandering around in the jungle and they knew a saber-toothed tiger was out there waiting to pounce on them. Their heart rate would be up, their senses were heightened, they were on "alert status" at all times, on the lookout for danger.

His boss was the woolly mammoth lurking in the jungle.

Now, hypervigilance is not in and of itself a bad thing. It's good for us when we're on the highway, say, or when we're in the pilot's seat, landing a 747. If you're in a foxhole, it's a good state to be in; it'll keep you very aware of danger. But if you're in that frame of mind day-in and day-out, month after month, sitting at your desk doing your expense reports with your body tensed in preparation for an attack by a saber-toothed tiger, your body is going to rebel.

And as I walk around the corporate world, I feel like my friend's state of mind is more the norm than the exception. People are scared and they're in denial. They're always on alert status, looking around the corner for danger. Their muscles are tensed and ready to run. But as we all know, it's probably easier to face a saber-toothed tiger than the Executive Vice President of Downsizing, Merging, and Re-employing. At least you can run from the tiger.

Most people I see in the workplace walk around with a fear that if they tell the truth about how they really feel about their job and their employer, they'll be fired. So they pretend that everything is fine, and they go more deeply and deeply into denial, and they twitch.

Stress in the workplace can cause severe health problems. Researchers now believe that everything from high blood pressure to ulcers to cancer can be caused by high levels of anxiety and stress. Complicating matters healthwise is that often when people are stressed at work and feeling exhausted and taken advantage of, they turn to activities that are bad for them: they overeat, they drink, they smoke. They can't sleep.

What ultimate effect is all of this going to have on the American workforce? How long can we continue to have the hardest working, and one of the least healthy, workforces in the world? For how long can people be living lives full of stress and anxiety and remain productive? I can't believe that in the long run this is going to pay off for anybody.

Our society needs to go back to one in which an authentic life can be brought into the workplace. And, indeed, there are many progressive companies out there today who are trying to do just that. There are companies where family members are really encouraged to take part in the workplace environment, either through on-site daycare or open houses or a simple nurturing of their employees' familial needs. They not only allow their employees to take real vacations and lunch hours, they insist on it.

And there are companies that value a physical environment in which the body's need for things like natural light and fresh air are a real consideration. Places where people wear the clothes that they feel comfortable wearing.

It's not easy to find these companies or to have jobs in which you can be totally yourself, but it's critical to people's health that they start finding a way to bring some authenticity into their workday.

The best way, of course, is to laugh.

Remember me and Beverly and the dog crap?

To truly be able to laugh at what's going on is the true gift of life. It's cleansing. When you can really laugh, it washes away things, it makes you see things through a different lens. It purifies what's going on. That's as good as it gets: a great big hearty laugh is like jumping into the pool on a hot summer day. It refreshes, it lessens the pain, it makes you feel good again.

We have to stop listening to the rhetoric and start listening to our inner voices; we need to trust our instinct and our innate desire to live honestly and with integrity.

Virtually every company I consult for has a printed "mission statement" and virtually every one of those mission statements goes on and on about how they value people. And you know what? The employees of those companies snicker whenever they hear those words. Mission statement! Mishegoss!

If we really valued people, we'd:

❖ *Make sure that people took time with their families*

❖ *Make sure that they took a break every day at lunchtime, not worked through it*

❖ *Give them a day off now and then for no good reason—just because*

❖ *Cultivate an environment in which people can say what's on their mind and not be afraid*

❖ *Stop sending people to workshops on how to deal with difficult people. Send the difficult people to workshops on how to get along with cooperative people!*

As individuals, we need to keep our heads about us. We all know, at some level, that there's a whole lot of questionable honesty and insincerity in the workplace. Maybe someday we'll have workplaces that foster complete honesty as well as individuality, civility, and optimism, all the "positive psychology" values. But that's something we're all going to have to work very hard at to see in our lifetimes.

In the meantime, it will be a whole lot easier to survive in a hypocritical workplace if you recognize it, and at least understand it and make fun of it wherever it's possible. When you can lighten up and laugh about things, no matter how hard they might be, you're going to feel better.

For example: if I were sitting in a meeting listening to windbag after windbag drone on and on about facilitating this and synergizing that, I'd say to myself "what a pompous ass" and make sure to translate every word of his back into the English language when I responded. Or, even better, I might playfully respond by out-buzzwording his buzzwords. I'd speak for fifteen minutes about vertical integration and customer retention and strategic planning and interactive feedback, all while keeping a straight face and knowing, in my heart, that I was making fun of the whole scene.

Rebellion against dishonesty is good for the soul—even if you do it nowhere but inside your own head, or when you're alone and safe. If you're being sold a bill of goods, "We at Mammoth Corporation care about our employees," you'll stay a lot saner if you say to yourself very clearly and without any self-doubt: "You're full of crap. If you cared about employees you wouldn't schedule meetings to take place when we should be heading home to have dinner with our kids."

Find a way to laugh about it. Can you play a little game in your head and cast the people in your office as cartoon characters? Who's your boss most like: Homer Simpson? Mr. Slate from *The Flintstones*? Mr. Magoo? One of the Power Puff Girls? And the colleague who drives you crazy: Is she Cruella DeVille? Angelica from *Rugrats*? The Queen from *Snow White* who, in your version, asks, "mirror mirror on the wall, who's the most vice-presidential of all?"

My favorite way to deal with office stress is to picture the revenge of the righteous, like the day that the giant hand of God comes down from the ceiling, points at the head of the CEO and says "Are you the lying scum who says he cares about his employees? Come with me."

We also have to honor our family lives by keeping our work life separate, like our grandparents did. We have to do more than pay lip service to the fact that family comes first, we need to do all the little things that confirm for ourselves and for our family that we really mean it.

❖ *When it's mealtime with the family, no one answers the phone.*

❖ *When it's time with the kids, we don't bring along work to read, we pay attention and remain present.*

❖ *Laptop computers are for working when you travel, not for checking e-mail when you visit your grandmother.*

❖ *When you go on vacation, and you go for a hike, the cell phone stays home.*

We need to keep our worklife in balance with the rest of our life, or soon we won't HAVE a "rest of our life." Human beings were not created to be high-stress, high-achievers twenty-four hours a day. There's nothing we should be doing "24/7" except breathing.

We must balance our workday with other things that are important:

Do something physical: exercise, walk, dance, anything that can get our bodies active for a portion of the day. Getting the blood flowing to the brain stimulates better thinking, higher energy, and a more optimistic outlook.

We should eat, and do it in a way that nurtures us, physically and emotionally. Blindly ingesting something at our desks does nothing to improve our souls, and little to improve our nutrition. We need to honor the needs of our body and feed it something that it wants, and something that will make us feel good.

And we should have fun. Find any excuse to laugh. Make fun of the nonsense around you, no matter how desperate it may seem. A technique that I've talked about and written about before, but that never fails to work wonders, is to really get into it when you're feeling miserable. Take it to the limit. Create a little drama. When you feel like you're overworked, throw your head back and yell to the sky: "Why am I being tortured this way?" When you feel like you can't stand another minute, throw yourself to the ground and kick your heels like a two-year-old.

You'll be laughing in no time.

Take a Socrates Break.
Don't ask me; ask yourself:

❖ *When was the last time you took a week-long vacation without calling into the office?*

❖ *If you are promoted from Senior Vice President to Executive Vice President, will more people come to your funeral?*

❖ *Do you get out of the office and take a break at least once during the day?*

❖ *When you're spending time with children or family, does it feel to you like you're wasting time that could be spent working?*

❖ *What would happen if you laughed a loud, joyous, uproarious laugh in your workplace?*

❖ *Do you take any time during the workday to do something physical—to get your heartrate up and your blood flowing? If your answer is no—why not?*

❖ Think about your career and ask yourself: what is this contributing to my life, long term? Is it helping me to be more responsible, civil, loving, hopeful? Is it doing anything to make me a happier person?

❖ Do you dread a visit from your boss, or look forward to it?

❖ When you're sitting at your desk, close your eyes for a moment and think: is it a place that feels comfortable, reassuring, encouraging of creativity? Or does it feel threatening, intimidating and unyielding?

❖ How much will your 401(k) be worth to you if you're sitting in a chair somewhere, dribbling?

3

Take a Walk and Eat a Tomato

*On caring for our bodies sensibly,
not obsessively*

WE ALL KNOW FROM THE TIME WE'RE KIDS in the playground that exercise is good for us. But current statistics from the American Heart Association show that only 22 percent of American adults are getting enough exercise to achieve cardiac fitness. Fifty-four percent get some exercise, but not enough to protect their hearts. And 24 percent of Americans over eighteen years of age get no exercise at all.

That means they never break a sweat, never get their lungs filled or their heart warmed up, never stretch their muscles or their tendons. Never *play*.

All I hear on TV and in ads is that people are obsessed with exercise. You'd think that all day long people were doing nothing but kickboxing and spinning, and that we were quickly on our way to becoming a society in which everyone looks like Jennifer Aniston and Brad Pitt. I mean, that's all you see in ads, right? People with perfectly chiseled bodies in form-fitting workout gear, running on a beach with a CD player plugged into their heads?

By now, with all the talk of people exercising more and the explosion in the number of gyms around the country, and the dozens of brands of workout shoes you see in stores, you'd expect to see pretty fit people walking around. You'd think we'd all be toned and oiled and buffed and ready for action. The truth is that "diet and exercise are unnatural acts," says Richard L. Atkinson, M.D., president of the American Obesity Association. "When our ancestors were lucky enough to find food, what did they do? They ate as much as they could, then lay down and went to sleep. I tell my patients that if they want to lose weight they have to be prepared to do unnatural acts for the rest of their lives— avoid fun foods and get lots and lots of exercise." This is a tough assignment for the overweight half of America.

That's pretty obvious. Take a good look. Instead of the sleek and toned people squeezed into their Michelle Pfeiffer Catwoman clothes that we see on TV, most people we see on the street can barely squeeze into their stretch sweatpants and nylon mu-mus.

And in our society, how could it be otherwise? Because the truth is, despite all the talk about exercise, the thing we are being sold today, more than anything else, is convenience. Most of the advances technology has made in our day-to-day lives contribute to our moving less and less. We have drive-thru everything, from express cleaners to restaurants to banks. You go to Hertz and they drive you right to the door of your rental car. We have valet parking at the mall. We can order anything we need over the Internet and have it delivered to our front door. And why do people take advantage of these services? Because it's easier. When we're all so overworked and exhausted, it's awfully enticing to take advantage of the thing that's easier. In fact, things have gotten so easy that we often find ourselves losing patience over the smallest things. Think about it. Our ancestors used to go out and plow the back forty, and we complain when it takes more than three minutes to get our food while sitting on our butts at Burger King's drive-thru window.

Everything today is about convenience. It's about making things easy on our tired bones. We take elevators and escalators whenever we can, even if we're only going up one flight. Airports now are equipped with moving side-walks because we're all so tired that the effort of moving the muscles in our legs to walk the distance of a few blocks is too trying on people.

We have home delivery of every pleasure known to man, from pizzas to books to videos to Häagen-Dazs ice cream. Who's not going to take advantage of such a plea-sure? We come home from work, it's late, we're tired. We dial a telephone and all we have to do is walk from the re-clining chair to the front door to get something we want. And, in many instances, that thing we want is full of fat and bursting with calories. I personally find myself looking for french fries and baby back ribs when I'm feeling stressed out. It's rare that I crave a tofu bar.

We can blame mother nature for at least part of our desire to pig out. She originally designed our bodies to require pounds and pounds of food. In prehistoric times, a 150-pound woman used about 1,600 calories a day just to dig up and chase down food, requiring about 3,000 calories daily just to stay alive. To counter high-calorie needs with mostly low-calorie offerings, the body evolved complex systems to defend against weight loss and maintain weight gain, including clinging to every ounce of consumed fat. As well as giving us superb fat-storing skills, mother nature also bestowed the human body with some fifty chemicals (galanin, serotonin, neuropeptides, endorphins and stress hormones) that not only drive our cravings for fat but reinforce bingeing behavior by leaving us feeling euphoric afterward.

We've all been trained these days to feel like we're disgraceful gluttons if we like to eat a brownie now and then, but what we're doing is simply acting on our biological imperative. The problem doesn't come from eating things that are pleasurable, it comes from the deadly combination of eating too many things that are pleasurable (because getting them is too easy), and not getting enough exercise for our bodies to compensate.

We've become a society of overeaters, often without our even being conscious of it. Think of these few small details: in 1957 the average fast-food hamburger contained one ounce of meat; today it contains six ounces. In 1957, the average bakery muffin weighed one-and-a-half ounces; now it weighs between five and eight ounces. In 1957, an average portion of popcorn you'd buy at the movies contained three cups. Now it contains sixteen cups.

Restaurant portions of food are enormous, and on average have a higher fat content than the food we eat at home. They have a higher fat content because, of course, that makes them taste better. And when the food tastes good, you'll want to go to that restaurant again.

The food service industry—just like every other industry—has created a world in which we are constantly tempted and seduced. Why not have a muffin? It's just a muffin (ignore that it's as big as a hot air balloon). It's just a little popcorn at the movie theater (even if it could serve a family of twelve for a week. And the drink that comes with it looks like a wading pool.) But of course what's really happening is that in order to keep us wanting more, the portions and the fat content keep increasing.

Today's average meal often contains *double* the number of calories that a normal meal contained for our grandparents. And we can't be blamed for wanting to eat meals like that. We've been fattened up for the kill by people who profit from the sale of food. And then the media makes us feel inadequate and lazy because we're not built like Olympic athletes.

We always seem astounded when we hear that the French, whose diet consists of a high level of fat, have a lower incidence of heart disease than we Americans. But think about it: their ice cream cones are the size of golf balls, ours are the size of tennis balls!

And, since these days the majority of us spend our working hours in sedentary office jobs, with hours of commuting time spent sitting in cars or trains, and since we spend so much of our free time watching television or surfing the Internet, how the hell are we ever going to get rid of those extra calories? Well, you probably know the answer. It's not easy, and from all signs out there, it's getting harder.

Do you know that 53 percent of adults are overweight? And do you find it amazing that there are twice as many obese people now than in the year 1900? No one ever heard of aerobics classes, much less Pilates or hydraulic cross-training machines, in the year 1900. But they were fit and we're all looking like rejects from *Babe: Pig in the City*.

We all talk about exercise, but so few of us ever feel like we have the time or the desire to do it on top of everything else that we're doing in the course of a day.

And, to be frank, I'm amazed that even those who do regularly exercise manage to do it. Our culture has made it so intimidating to exercise that most normal people with normal bodies—and particularly people who have never exercised in a gym before—are terrified to start. Think of the ads you see for gyms. Who are those models? Do they really need to find women who look like Linda Hamilton in *Terminator II*? Or men with thighs more chiseled than Michelangelo's *David*? How often do you see people who actually have bodies like that in the real world? (And could you tell me where, exactly?) But they show us perfection; they'd never show someone who looks like my grandmother Francesca squeezed into a leotard.

So, to start, people are intimidated and self-conscious about going to the gym because they think everyone else will look like Ben Affleck or Madonna, spend seven hours on the StairMaster without breaking a sweat, and make fun of their pitiful and flabby attempts to do a leg-lift.

And then, of course, there's the anxiety-provoking phenomenon of figuring out what to wear. Have you tried to buy a pair of sneakers lately? If you have, you've discovered, like me, that there's no such thing. Sneakers don't exist anymore. You go into a store to buy a pair of sneakers, and there's a wall of fifty different kinds of "workout shoes." What do you want? Tennis shoes? Running shoes? Walking shoes? Hiking shoes? Basketball shoes? Aerobics? Cross trainers? Outdoors? Indoors? And what brand is best for you? Nike? New Balance? Adidas? Converse? Reebok? Suppose I start out on a walk and suddenly decide to break into a jog? Do I have to stop and change shoes? What do I carry them in? And suppose it starts to rain and I have to move my outdoor workout indoors? Do I need four pairs of shoes? Do I need to get a pair of Nike indoor runners and Easy Spirit outdoor walkers and Reebok indoor walkers and New Balance outdoor runners? What happens if I forget and wear my indoor runners when I go for a walk outside? Will I blow up? Will I suffer "foot trauma?"

Four pairs of "workout shoes"—that's three hundred and twenty five dollars. Forget foot trauma, that's financial trauma! But it's really beside the point because unless you really know what you're doing, or unless you're in a store where the salespeople really know what *they're* doing (and what are the chances of that?), you've probably left the store feeling confused and annoyed.

And that's just the start. Your feet!

What about your clothes? Should they be a material that stretches or a material that confines? Should it be breathing material or a material that makes you sweat? Can it be loose and comfortable and hide some of your problem spots, or do you have to climb into it with a winch and be vacuum-sealed like the foods the astronauts eat?

Before you've even walked in the door of a gym, you've had reason for intense stress and self-consciousness. Just the particulars of figuring out what to wear turns off a huge percentage of new exercisers.

But let's say you're one of the intrepid ones and you've actually managed to buy shoes and a t-shirt. When you get to the gym, what should you do?

Well, for me, I thought maybe I'd get on a treadmill for a little while, and then take a class.

Forget it! Just to get on a treadmill you need to pass your instrument flying certification from the FAA. Have you ever seen so many dials and buttons and contraptions? I just wanted to run a little, and next thing I know I'm in what looks like the cockpit of a 747 ready for takeoff.

There are StairMasters and StepMasters and elliptical cross trainers and hydraulic contraptions that scared the hell out of me just looking at them. I wasn't sure if I was about to get a workout or an M.R.I.

So I thought, OK, maybe it's me. Maybe I need the human touch. No machines, I'm going to take a class. So I look at the class schedule.

First at 6 A.M. there's Pilates, followed at seven by Spinning. At eight it's time for Cardio Kickboxing, Stepping at nine followed by Kombat Cardio, where they use an object the size and shape of an M-16 to train the shoulders. I showed up at eleven, just in time for the Firefighter's Workout in which two working Boston firemen led a class of participants climbing ladders with hoses on their backs, dragging 125-pound dummies across the floor. Is this exercising, or are we in training for Armageddon? Before the class was over I was back home, waiting for Oprah to come on with an eight-ounce Morning Glory muffin in my hands.

Why does it have to be so intimidating? Exercise, like virtually everything else in our society, has been so overhyped and over-marketed that it ends up feeling, to most people, like something you need to be an expert at in order to do properly.

Our society has moved physical activity out of something that we do on a day-to-day basis and moved it into a little ritualized world in which we have to dress, move and sweat in exactly the right way or risk self-conscious embarrassment.

Imagine what our grandparents would have thought of StairMasters (**Stunata! Why don't they just go up and down the stairs fifty times a day like me?**) or latex workout gear.

This is a big "duh."

There's a reason we're born with limbs. They're supposed to move. They *need* to move. And they need to move more than just three times a week when we put on special neon-colored clothes and stand on a machine that looks like the command cabin of the Space Shuttle *Atlantis*.

The active use of our physical bodies has got to be more a part of our everyday lives. We need to get into the habit of using our bodies every minute by engaging our bodies in work, in play, in our errands, in all our daily rituals.

It's crazy for us to think that we can take a class a few times a week

> WHEN NATURE CREATED OUR BODIES, WE DIDN'T HAVE THE OPTION TO "SUPERSIZE OUR FRIES." IF WE WANTED TO EAT MORE, WE HAD TO CATCH AND KILL AN ANIMAL, OR CLIMB MORE TREES.

and the rest of the time ride elevators and use valet parking and buy our meals in drive-thrus.

Think of our grandparents. Even if they weren't doing physical labor (though many more of them were, certainly, than we are now), they were walking. They were chopping vegetables. They were washing clothes by hand. They were climbing stairs. In 1900, the average person burned four thousand calories per day. Today, the average is half that.

I know it's a cliche, but when they were kids, our grandparents walked to school. Now, even for adolescents who live less than one mile from their school, two-thirds of them drive or are driven. Less than a mile! Not only that, 75 percent of adolescents do not even meet the standard of having regular "light to moderate" physical activity. Our teenagers are couch potatoes! And they're suffering from the same issues as the rest of the population. Most of them get chauffeured around to school and to social events. They grab their meals on the go at the mall or the local Pizzeria Uno.

Kids use their parents as role models, and most parents are always talking about how tired they are. I've actually heard people say to kids "stop moving around so much, you're making me tired!" Excuse me? How can you get tired just watching someone else move? Or is that you're feeling guilty because you're not moving yourself?

We need to encourage, not discourage. When kids fidget, fidget along with them. And how's this for encouragement? A recent study described in *Science* magazine suggests that chronic mini-movements (or fidgeting!) may play a tremendous role in weight management. Mayo Clinic researchers deliberately overfed volunteers by one thousand calories a day. Predictably, some gained a great deal of weight, but others gained hardly any. It turned out that the latter group fidgeted away up to 850 calories a day, equivalent to an 8.5 mile walk.

I've taught myself to fidget! I'll purposely walk around the house when I'm talking on the phone, I'll get up every thirty minutes or so when I'm writing and walk around the yard. I'll even get down on the floor and do a few leg lifts. Now, I'm sure a few of you are thinking "I can't do that at the office!" But I'm sure you can think of something to take advantage of these benefits. If you can't walk in the yard, go to the water fountain several times each morning. You need to make it fun. Make it a game.

Today's workout fascists would have us believe that

there are precise rules for efficient walking. It'll make you crazy. Do I keep my arms up? My arms down? Do I pump? Do I swivel? Do I twist? Do I lift my knees or keep my knees even? Should I bend at the ankle or not?

Who cares?

Sometimes I go for a walk and pretend that I'm in a marching band, just cause I think it's fun. Sometimes I jump around and throw my fists up in the air like Sylvester Stallone at the end of *Rocky*. Sometimes I kick my legs like I'm one of the Rockettes.

I do things that keep me interested and entertained, and I don't really give a damn if anybody else thinks I'm doing it wrong, or that I look ridiculous. I *know* I look ridiculous. Isn't it wonderful? I'm alive!

And you know what? I usually end up not only having a good workout, but also having fun and talking to people. Because most people really, in their hearts, wish that they were having as much fun working out as it looks like I'm having! So we start laughing together and before long I'm leading a conga line around the park.

Eat to Lose

The other thing we need to do, of course, is develop saner eating habits. That's not an easy thing to do when everything around you is *in*sane.

There's so much information being given to us all the time about how to eat in a healthier manner that you'd think some of it would make sense. You'd think that if you read two books, or two articles, you'd see the same information again and again.

But no, that would be too helpful to the human race.

Instead, every time we read an article, a magazine, or a book about eating healthy or starting a diet program, we're given conflicting information.

Low carbs! High protein! Everybody's talking about a low-carb high-protein diet. Everyone says that's the thing that works. That's how to lose weight and get in control and be healthy. Everywhere you turn, there's another story about how a low-carb diet is good for you. Eating the beef, chicken, fish and fats offered on the diet increases the stores of energy, makes you feel more full, and reduces the production of a certain insulin hormone that makes it easier to lose weight. *Great. I'm starting a low-carb diet today*.

Then you read another magazine, and it tells you that a low-carb diet will kill you. It makes the case that our body *needs* carbs, needs the fast energy, and that restricting carbohydrates depletes the glycogen stored in the muscles, which makes you weaker and makes movement and exercise more difficult. Some doctors believe that the high fat and protein consumption suggested on most low-carb diets cause liver and kidney problems.

There goes my diet plan.

For a few years now, we've been told that eating a high-fiber diet was an effective dietary defense against cancer, particularly colon cancer. So, since we human beings tend to dutifully try to do what's best for our health, everyone started eating fiber. Lots of fiber. Oat bran in everything. People were so stuffed up with fiber they didn't go to the toilet for a month. When they finally did, they passed a wicker chair.

Just recently, the results of a new study were released, and it said that maybe fiber doesn't really have an effect on colon cancer after all.

Now they tell me, after 974 bowls of All-Bran.

It's another manifestation of the information overload. As soon as a couple of scientists come out of their lab and announce the results of a study with fifteen patients that say some food item *might*, under certain circumstances, have an effect on health, the news media releases the information (often in an exploitative fashion: "tonight at ten, can a rutabaga cure cancer?"). Then, the machine starts working. Everywhere you turn for a week, there's another article about rutabaga and cancer. No magazine or newspaper or talk show can skip the story, because, of course, it's good for ratings. People like to hear good news. So, within a few weeks it's all anyone is talking about. Every time you run into someone at the supermarket they ask "did you eat your rutabaga today? They're very good for you, you know."

And because, let's face it, people are concerned about their health and don't want to take chances, they don't just listen to the stories, they start buying and eating rutabagas. Sales of rutabagas go through the roof. The rutabaga farmers go into triple time. They can't keep up with the demand, so rutabagas start being imported from South America.

Within a month, if you go to the supermarket you'll

not only find more rutabagas than bananas on the produce aisle, you'll start seeing regular products, like Cheerios, with big swipes across the front of the box: **"NOW WITH RUTABAGA!"**

You'll be able to buy dried rutabaga, rutabaga shampoo, a copy of *The Rutabaga Cure* in paperback on the checkout line, and, to drink, a new flavor from Snapple: Rockin' Rutabaga.

A month later, of course, another study is released that says under certain circumstances rutabagas may in fact cause impotence. Rockin' Rutabaga is pulled from the shelves.

We're so confused about what to eat! And who could blame us? There are no clear signals, and everyone is trying to market things with the claim that they're healthy. Everywhere we turn, products are labeled **Organic! Low Fat! High in Fiber! High in Vitamin C! Now with Ginkgo-Biloba!**

It used to be that doctors told us what nutrients to take. Now we just choose for ourselves, based on what we read in magazines and hear on the *Today Show*. In fact, I think I should be given an honorary doctorate of nutrition for all I know about vitamins and minerals from watching those TV shows!

We all run around acting like doctors, because we are given so much detailed information about what things are healthy or unhealthy. But of course, I don't know half of what I need to know to understand the full consequences of herbs and minerals on the body. I know that. But many people don't pay nearly as much attention as they should before they put these substances into their bodies. People read things like "Vitamin E is good for your heart" so they go to a health food store and buy a Vitamin E supplement. There it is, health in a pill. And since we're all in

> IF MOTHER NATURE WANTED US TO TAKE VITAMIN SUPPLEMENTS, THERE'D BE TREES GROWING WITH LITTLE CAPSULES ON THEM INSTEAD OF ORANGES.

our basic natures trusting souls, we think that since these pills are being sold over the counter that they can't hurt us.

Wrong!

Yes, some studies show that Vitamin E may reduce the risk of heart attacks and atherosclerosis. So it may be good for us. But the key word is *may*. Vitamin E acts as a blood thinner, just like aspirin. Under most circumstances, that's believed to be a good thing. But what is not well-known is that if you are on certain medications that also act to thin your blood, then taking Vitamin E in addition to that drug may well thin your blood *too much*. If our blood is too thin, it can cause internal bleeding or a host of other problems.

Similarly, Echinacea is a very commonly used herbal supplement that people take to relieve cold symptoms. You can buy it in any supermarket, drug store, or health food store. Some bottles carry the very important warning that Echinacea should not be used by pregnant women or by people with autoimmune disorders. Others do not. Why do we treat a substance that could prove harmful to people, and particularly to unborn babies, in such a cavalier fashion?

Remember that just because something is purported to be good for your health, you do not have to overdose on it. Just because it comes in a capsule doesn't mean more is better. We seem to think that if Vitamin C, D, or B is good for us, we should take the maximum recommended amount. The irony is that we all know that broccoli, tomatoes, spinach, etc. are good for us—but how often do we hear someone say "I took my broccoli this morning; just one more pound before the day is over!"? No. Pills are in.

We as a nation naively believe that if something is being sold in stores as good for us, it must really be good for us. We have to question that. It seems to me that the issue of the craziness associated with vitamin supplements, and with eating crazes spurred on by medical claims, boils down to the same issue: we all have good intentions about eating the things we believe are healthy. We want to do the things that we're told are good for our body.

But we're being misled. People and corporations who can profit from our desire for good health are marketing products to us that may or may not be helpful, and can often be harmful, to us.

But here's the big "duh." It's pretty obvious that virtually everything being touted as a wonder supplement is available in the everyday food we eat. If we simply ate a healthy balanced diet like our grandmothers did, we wouldn't need any of this crap.

People take beta-carotene supplements to improve their eyesight. Our grandmothers told us to eat carrots and we'd see better at night. What's in a carrot? **Beta-carotene!**

Our grandmothers told us to drink milk for strong bones. Now we take calcium supplements for strong bones. What's in milk? Calcium, of course.

The human body was designed to eat a balanced diet. We survived in the caves by eating mainly fruits, vegetables and grains. We also ate small quantities of protein and dairy (since they were harder to get).

Grandma Francesca ate a classic Mediterranean diet—a lot of vegetables, pasta and bread, some fish, a little meat, olive oil as the primary fat, and yes, she even ate cheese. After the meal, a small dolci-a sweet—for dessert. Maybe she didn't look like Gwyneth Paltrow, but she looked pretty good, and she was healthy. She lived to be ninety-seven, and she died with all her own teeth and no cavities.

Food is so much better for us than vitamins or supplements. Not only do we get the minerals we

---

The Tombstone No One Wants #3

HERE LIES JANE DOE.

FOUR DAYS A WEEK SHE WORKED OUT TO AN EXERCISE ROUTINE SHE HATED; AND SHE ONLY ATE FOODS THAT SHE BELIEVED WERE GOOD FOR HER— BUT THAT SHE DIDN'T REALLY ENJOY. HERE SHE IS ANYWAY.

need in much healthier more appropriate quantities, without the possible consequences of misdosage, we get so many more nutrients than we could have otherwise. Sure, we can take a lutein supplement, but how about a tomato instead? Then we get not only lutein, but lycopene, an antioxident nutrient, and high levels of vitamins C and A, plus a little potassium and a little iron.

We get a unique mix of minerals inside every food, a mix that is more complex and better for our bodies than popping some pills. The fact is that we still have no idea what effect the particular mix of ingredients inside a food may have on the body. If Mother Nature knows her stuff (and as far as I can see, she comes up the winner every time), there are added benefits built in to the *combination* of nutrients that comprise a tomato when compared against a similar amount of the same nutrients taken separately. No mix of vitamin supplements will give you all the nutritional riches of a well-rounded meal.

Do I think you might benefit from vitamin supplementation? Maybe. But before you start dosing, make sure the person who is advising you, if anyone, is credible. Do your homework. You wouldn't take medication without consulting a physician (I hope!). Don't take supplements without a similar level of care and scrutiny.

Honoring Our Bodies

Use your common sense. You know you have to move. You know that moving is better than not moving, and that sweating is better than not sweating. If you don't do it exactly the same way that Madonna does it, so what? If you're doing more than you used to do, or you're doing the amount that's right for you, congratulate yourself.

Exercise is good for you and what it does for you is to take stress out of your body. If all the nonsense surrounding it makes you feel more uneasy and more stressful because it's intimidating . . . move on.

It's a simple process. Move. Breathe. Break a sweat. Keep it up. Don't let it get too complicated.

Believe it or not, at age sixty I have taken up playing racquetball. My friends think I'm nuts and several of them have reserved advance seats for the funeral. But I'm having the time of my life.

It's fun. I've spent half my life inside gyms, it seems, and now that I've discovered this game, I never want to get on a StairMaster again as long as I live. I still lift weights for power and strength and I stretch (I'm trying to get taller!).

Racquetball (and other competitive sports) keeps you sharp, alert and entertained. It honors the inborn desire to play that no one had to teach us when we were children. Human beings like to play, they like to run, jump, tumble, catch, throw and all the things that we see six-year-olds do in the playground without any prompting whatsoever.

Think of the effect on your entire being of a half-hour of play versus another half hour on the StairMaster. Yes, the StairMaster may burn off as many calories, or even more calories, but what effect does the tedium have on the brain and the muscles? We don't know. But whenever I see a row of people on those machines, all looking up at the bank of TVs with headphones in their ears, I realize that they are distracting themselves from the exercise they are getting. That spirit of distraction, or of denial, of where they are and what they are doing, must have a detrimental effect. We are all complete beings, our minds and our bodies are one interrelated unit, and engaging both in the same activity has a beneficial effect on both.

Exercising should be fun, it should engage the brain. Games keep our bodies AND our brains active. **We need to get into the game of life!**

And, on a day-to-day basis, we need to get more physical in the little things we do. Grandma Francesca never played racquetball, but she'd walk everywhere she went. And she'd carry big bags of groceries. It was a very physical life: lifting, pulling, walking, bending, sweeping. She spent part of most days gardening, she grew tomatoes and then she would pick them and pound them and bottle the sauce. She was always kneading the bread, pounding the veal cutlets. Her muscles were strong.

If you have to go to the store and buy a newspaper, walk. If there's a stairway at the mall as well as an escalator, take the stairs. Instead of plopping into an easy chair after dinner and allowing your kids to sit right there next to you, get the whole family moving; walk to the park, walk around your own backyard, for God's sake! Do family aerobics (I know it sounds ridiculous, but what the hell? Be ridiculous!). Let the neighbors look out their windows and see the whole family doing leg lifts in the backyard! Dance down the street like a Broadway chorus line. The next time you're tempted to sit through another episode of *Who Wants to be a Millionaire* or to slog through more work from your briefcase, put the CD of "Livin' La Vida Loca" on the stereo and dance your buns off! and if it all makes you feel too silly, stop thinking! Or pretend it's not about you at all (and think of how good it is for your kids).

In addition to the public displays, think about the little ways you can move more and sit less. Can you stand at your desk instead of sitting all day? Can you get one of those headset telephones and stretch while you return your phone calls? How about walking up the stairs to your boss's office instead of taking the elevator?

Exercising and eating should be natural pleasures, not obsessive and intimidating tasks in which we feel pressure to "do the right thing". If we look down deep into our souls, we know that exercise is best for us when it is fun, when it's something we love to do, when we want to keep at it for as long as we can, not when we're looking at our watches and counting the minutes until it's over. What's better for our bodies and our souls, an afternoon of hiking through the woods, or sixty minutes on the treadmill at level twenty-seven? A few hours kayaking on a sundrenched lake, or an hourlong session on the rowing machine? Putting on a pair of old shorts and a t-shirt and heading down to a local park for a game of basketball with friends, or pulling into lycra stretchwear for a trip around the air conditioned, florescent-lit steel workout circuit at the gym?

The answer is a simple one, and one that you've probably heard over and over again: **moderation**. It's not something that our society values. We're a society of people that tends to binge and then fast; that sits like couch potatoes for a month, then decides to train for a marathon.

It's the obsession that is killing us, in both directions. When we don't give ourselves enough room to have a pastry now and then (or whatever our craving is), we reinforce the feeling that life is cruel and unyielding. We get depressed, and ultimately binge on that thing we crave. Similarly, if we feel like a sloth because one day we fall short of two hours on the treadmill at a 45 percent incline at level 10—we're going to ultimately have to rebel against that feeling of guilt or go crazy. Nobody can be perfect all the time.

That doesn't mean we shouldn't set goals for ourselves. Of course we should. But they must be achievable goals, and we need to be soft on ourselves if we fall short one day; and we have to be proud of ourselves if we overachieve the next day. Life is not strictly measured. It should be fun! Eat what makes you feel good, but just enough. Work out until you feel strong, but not so much that you risk injury.

The best way to monitor if you're eating and exercising properly is to pay close attention to how you feel. Life creates energy, and your body runs on an energy that you can feel, if you pay attention.

If you wake up tired, and find that you're pushing yourself through the day, dragging along and plopping into chairs at every opportunity—that's a message to you. You're doing something wrong. You need to eat differently, or exercise differently. Try different combinations until your energy changes.

You need to rate yourself closely. On a scale of one to ten, how is your energy? And what sorts of energy are you feeling? Are you feeling peppy? Exuberant? Sharp? Wild? Powerful?

I know that some mornings I wake up and I feel great and know that my energy balance is right. Other times I'll wake up—not too often, happily—and I'll feel tired and draggy. There's always a reason: did I eat too many carbohydrates? Did I drink too much alcohol? Did I not have enough fun yesterday? Did I not get enough exercise? Did I get too much exercise?

Your energy level is your foundation for a good attitude and a happy life. Keep it burning brightly and you can do anything.

Take a Socrates Break. Don't ask me, ask yourself:

❖ *Do you spend more time dressing for the gym than working out there? Do you choose your workout outfit with the same care you use choosing a cocktail dress?*

❖ *How do you feel when you are in the middle of whatever exercise you do most regularly: as if you could happily continue to do it for as long as you like, or are you counting the seconds until it's over?*

❖ Do you often change your eating habits based on what you read or hear about the latest nutritional studies?

❖ Do you feel bad when you see someone who is a "perfect specimen"? Does that intimidate you, inspire you, or simply enrage you with its unfairness?

❖ Do you tend to eat whatever portion of food is given to you, assuming that it is the proper amount to eat, or do you make that determination on your own?

❖ Do you take vitamin or herbal supplements without really researching the medical effects they could have on your body? Would you take a prescription drug without the advice of doctor?

❖ Do you like to talk about, or even just take note of, how little you ate, and act as if it's something to be proud of?

❖ Are you aware of the nutritional counts of everything you put in your mouth? Has that helped you feel happier and more balanced?

❖ Do you take an elevator, escalator, or a "moving sidewalk" when you could easily walk? Why?

❖ Do you ever finish a meal and actually try to stop and think, how do I feel? Do I feel satisfied? Nurtured? Do I feel disappointed and cheated? Do I feel energetic? Or do I feel lethargic?

4

Who Wants to Be an Idiot?

On mass media and choice

A FEW MONTHS AGO, as I wrote this, our society reached a new low when the Fox network aired a special television show called *"Who Wants to Marry a Millionaire?"* I'm sure you're aware of it and I don't have to describe it in great detail, but just in case you happened to be traveling in Fiji for six months around the time of this fabulous broadcast, here's what you need to know. The show's producers advertised for women to come forward and compete to see who would be chosen, during the course of an hour-long television show, to marry a man they'd never seen before. The man, of course, happened to be very rich.

I doubt there would have been much turnout for *"Who Wants to Marry a Hot Dog Vendor"*—but who the hell knows anymore?

So this rich guy gets to choose among fifty finalists who

prance across the stage in front of him like contestants in a beauty pageant (which, in a way, I guess this was . . .) except at the end of this show, instead of a crown and a bouquet of roses, the winner gets to take home a wedding ring and a new groom and the promise of "till death do us part." Just like that!

Listen to this: 23 million people watched this fiasco. At the same time, a debate was going on between the Republican candidates for president of the United States. Three million people watched that.

Among women aged eighteen to thirty-four, it was the most-watched program ever aired on the network.

Now, is it *me*, or is this the most insane thing you ever heard? I thought I was dreaming when I heard this story. I still think it's a bad dream.

First: who the hell are the fifty women who would be so willing to publicly embarrass themselves in front of millions of people and parade in front of a wealthy would-be husband like the mail-order brides of centuries ago? These were not poor women from undeveloped countries, mind you, they were successful and attractive women, most of whom had good careers.

Next: What is with this guy, the groom, to want to debase himself this way and, effectively, admit to the world that he can't find a wife the old-fashioned way? By meeting someone and charming her until he wins her love? You'd think a multimillionaire would have other options (A kicker to the story is that, later, it was discovered that there was an outstanding restraining order against him based on an allegation that he hit a previous girlfriend. *Maybe that's what made it harder for him to date women.*

Next, and perhaps most importantly: why the hell did 23 million of us watch this ludicrous and disgusting display? I'd like to give people the benefit of the doubt and believe that they tuned in simply because the event was so massively stupid and surreal that they wanted to see if it would really happen; that maybe they hoped it was some kind of enormous prank and that when they tuned in, an executive of Fox Television would be on the air telling them that, of course, no one was going to marry a stranger and that, of course, a corporation of their reputation and stature would never debase themselves to broadcast such a thing. It was all a joke. Here, now, a new production of *King Lear*.

But, no. It was all too real—and millions of people really seemed to want to watch this profoundly cynical, packaged-for-television, corporately-sanctioned and sold-by-the-minute wedding purely for its entertainment value.

But that wasn't bad enough!

Several days later, when all was said and done and the wedding was annulled after the groom's blemished history was revealed, then the truly surreal things started to happen. The bride, Darva Conger, a thirty-four-year-old veteran of the Persian Gulf War and an emergency room nurse, became an instant celebrity. She was interviewed by Diane Sawyer on *Good Morning America*; her story was broadcast on *20/20*; she was on the *Today Show* and virtually every other television news show on the air. Interviewed by countless newspapers and magazines, she became a national celebrity.

This happens again and again. Some jerk does something (often something incredibly dumb or even illegal) that makes the media take notice. That gives them their fifteen minutes of fame. Then they cash in, and we all watch until the next one comes along. Amy Fisher, Lorraine and John Wayne Bobbitt, Jessica Hahn, Darva Conger. The list goes on. As I write this, it's Richard Hatch, the guy who ate rats and betrayed his friends on TV's *Survivor*. What have these people accomplished other than to make asses of themselves? Why do we care? And why do we watch?

I think I know why, but it's a sad statement on how we live today.

I think that in today's society people are so exhausted, so lonely, so separated from other people who are important to them, that they look to television and celebrities to fill that void. The human brain requires involvement and attachment to other people. So, instead of getting involved in the lives of our families and our neighbors the way our grandparents did, we get involved in the lives of people like Richard Hatch. Television presents us with "real" people whose lives we can relate to and, in a funny way, with whom we can feel attached. It fulfills a biological imperative. And as for the people who allow parts of their lives to be lived out on television, they achieve what so many people used to have to accomplish something astounding to achieve: fame.

They all seem to become national celebrities; they are

interviewed on every television network and are usually offered hundreds of thousands of dollars from magazines and tabloids for everything from life stories to nude photos. Then comes the autobiography and the made-for-TV movie.

So, yes, for people like Darva Conger and Richard Hatch and Amy Fisher, fame seems to have led to some sort of career in which they keep selling their one idiotic act of celebrity over and over. Amy Fisher published a book. Richard Hatch is making a fortune on the lecture circuit. Darva Conger posed nude for *Playboy*. Now, there's the pinnacle of success, right?

So is it any wonder that people stand outside studio windows and wave their arms, begging to be noticed? Or that people follow roving reporters around hoping for their moment in front of the camera? Or that people pull wacky and life-threatening stunts simply so they'll get publicity?

It's not surprising that people these days seem to think that being covered in the media— the most artificial of all experiences—is the thing that will make them whole. It's because media coverage brings fame, and fame brings hope for a

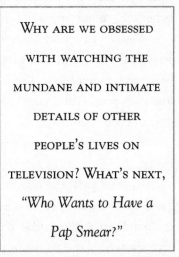

WHY ARE WE OBSESSED WITH WATCHING THE MUNDANE AND INTIMATE DETAILS OF OTHER PEOPLE'S LIVES ON TELEVISION? WHAT'S NEXT, *"Who Wants to Have a Pap Smear?"*

better life. Our society is so obsessed with fame and with media coverage that we are becoming creatures that crave the camera the way we should be craving intimacy; as if the way to propagate the species is to appear on *Oprah*.

Fame is seductive. But the real question, it seems to me, is this: people only get famous when the public makes them famous. In other words, there would be no such thing as fame if people stopped paying attention. Darva Conger and the other ordinary people who have captured the public's imagination for doing idiotic things are only famous because we watch them. If we stopped watching, the media would stop airing these ridiculous displays of humanity at its worst.

Why are we tuning in to see Darva Conger? Or Monica Lewinsky? Or Joey Buttafuoco? Or John Wayne Bobbitt? Can anyone explain to me why we seem to have a desire to watch people who gained a form of celebrity by doing unbelievably stupid things?

Monica Lewinsky has been on talk shows and in magazines talking about her struggle to lose weight. She has been paid, rumor has it, a million dollars, by Jenny Craig to lose forty pounds and keep it off, then to talk about it. Why does anybody care?

I've lost forty pounds; nobody's given me a damn thing!

In great part, the reason we watch these people is because these are the people who are presented to us. I find it profoundly disturbing that Diane Sawyer, and other elite broadcasters, chose to waste their time and ours by interviewing the likes of Darva Conger. What was she going to say? How many times could she be asked "why did you marry the other jerk on TV?" What profound thought is going to come out of this? Is there anything about this episode that could make anyone watching it, or

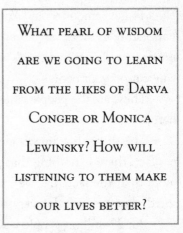

WHAT PEARL OF WISDOM ARE WE GOING TO LEARN FROM THE LIKES OF DARVA CONGER OR MONICA LEWINSKY? HOW WILL LISTENING TO THEM MAKE OUR LIVES BETTER?

participating in it, grow as a human being?

We have so many interesting people in this nation—people who do important things and make a difference in the world. People who are trying to feed the poor and create beautiful buildings and write magnificent music and perform amazing athletic feats. Why is some jerk who jumped off the Brooklyn Bridge being interviewed, and being enriched by, the national media, while researchers who are having breakthroughs in finding a cure for AIDS are toiling in obscurity?

In our grandparents' generation, the people who achieved fame were people we admired and looked up to. Amelia Earhart was famous for her groundbreaking flying; Albert Einstein was famous for his theory of relativity; Walt Disney was famous for creating Mickey Mouse, Snow White, and Disneyland. Those are the people who got famous, and the people whom we saw interviewed on television (once it existed) and on the radio.

To get famous today? You have to debase yourself on national television, have oral sex with the president, be a minor who shoots her lover's wife in the head, or have your wife cut off your penis.

These are the people who are presented as our national heroes.

The thing that amazes me most about all this is a simple fact: there is nothing that people these days talk about more than the fact that we have no time, that we're pressured, that we can't do everything that we want to do.

But 23 million people wasted an hour watching Darva Conger get married. Why?

Because the programmers and advertisers who control the television industry are very clever about creating programming that is simple, seductive and not very demanding. They know that when people are as exhausted as the American public is, the best way to capture their attention is to give them something that is captivating but effortless. After an exhausting day at work, and taking care of families, the last thing people need is anything that feels like another demand for them to perform.

So we are aggres-

WHY WOULD ANYONE CHOOSE TO WATCH MONICA LEWINSKY TALKING ABOUT HER WEIGHT PROBLEMS ON NATIONAL TELEVISION WHEN THEY COULD BE WATCHING *Casablanca* INSTEAD?

sively presented with simple fare that is easy to watch and that fills the voids in our lives.

We all know that the American public is overworked and feels underloved. Nobody has any time to see family anymore, to live out the rituals of life: the big Sunday dinners, the holiday weekends, the evenings around the kitchen table. Many of us work through meals, or certainly do some late-night work after dinner. Many of us don't have the time to play with our own children, much less our nieces, nephews, or neighbors' children.

Television programmers try to fill that void by putting simulated versions on TV. So now, we find ourselves watching people impersonating the real people we should be spending time with!

I remember the time when women actually sat around in their kitchens and talked together about the things that interested them. Now they watch *The View*. They can watch other women sit and have a coffee klatch while they sit at home all alone and think that, gee, that looks like fun.

I remember when families used to air their grievances with one another over the dining room table. Now they do it on *Jerry Springer*.

I remember when we

DON'T YOU FIND IT INFURIATING TO IMAGINE TELEVISION EXECUTIVES THINKING "I KNOW, PEOPLE DON'T HAVE TIME FOR THEIR FRIENDS ANYMORE. LET'S GIVE THEM *Friends!*?"

lived together in close proximity to our neighbors and our families, and we learned how to work out our problems and differences by discussion, argument, and mutual consideration, because these were the people we were stuck with. Now we watch groups of people thrown into artificial situations on shows like *Survivor* and *Big Brother* trying to live together the way we used to.

The problem with all of this, it seems to me, is twofold. First, the more we allow ourselves to buy into and feel satisfied by the sort of "faux" life that these television shows offer, the more separate and isolated we become. If watching conversational television fulfills our need for community, why should we communicate with real people about things happening in our own lives?

And second, given the fact that we have so little spare time in our lives for enriching experiences, don't we have to become far more selective about what we watch, and how often we watch it?

It's so important for our psychological health that we stimulate our brains with material that is engaging, that is energizing, that helps to excite our brains and enrich our souls. Major studies have been done that prove that certain sorts of stimulation increase the physical state of the dendrites and synapses in the brain. Intense and invigorating intellectual pursuits, like learning a language, studying music, or doing crossword puzzles, actually help keep the brain vital and alive.

There's no scientific basis for this, but I swear that watching Joey Buttafuoco talk about his women problems on TV didn't keep a single cell in anyone's brain alive. In fact, it probably helped kill a few.

In my grandparents' generation, free time at home was spent in ways that were enriching. I remember my grandfather would sit around in the evenings and listen to Italian opera on the radio; he would read Pirandello. Every day he'd go out and buy the Italian language newspaper and read every word. And he was not unusual in any way, or particularly well-educated or intellectual for his time. My grandfather wasn't a college professor or anything, he was an ordinary working man of his generation. In those years (in the absence of television), people spent their leisure time pursuing forms of entertainment that were enlightening and that stretched their intellect.

It's hard for people today to do that. In a society like ours that is so overworked and overstressed, when we finally stop working and want a few minutes to unwind, we do the thing that is easiest: We turn on the tube.

That's not necessarily so bad. Listen, there's a lot that's good to watch on TV (there's a particularly funny woman on PBS from time to time)—far be it from me to trash the medium. I think that there are some very important and powerful dramas being produced today. There are excellent documentaries and there is cultural programming, there's some brilliant cutting-edge comedy that is just plain cleverly entertaining and fun to watch, and there are talk shows that stimulate, enrich, and actually enhance people's lives.

The point is that we need to make intelligent choices about the way we are entertained. If we allow ourselves to get drawn into the seductive lowest-common-denominator programming that is very aggressively sold to us as entertainment, soon our intellect will be pulled down to the lowest common denominator!

By entertaining ourselves with things that are stimulating but not enriching—like million-dollar quiz shows or fight-fest talk shows—we increase our feelings of spiritual emptiness. We fall into a tempting trap: it's pleasurable to spend time in a mindless way. When your mind is engaged all day, every day, it's relaxing to let it be simply distracted, but not really entertained or challenged. But it's deadly. In our hearts, we all know that what we are doing with the time is, really, just wasting it away. How often have you even heard people use the phrase they "killed a few hours" watching television? I don't know about you, but I don't have enough hours on this planet to want to kill any of them!

Watching time-wasting television keeps us feeling isolated and shallow; it submerges us in a world that is base and vulgar and ends up making us feel less evolved. It mires us in mediocrity; we do nothing to help ourselves see that the world is full of awe and wonder and truly magnificent works of art and culture that could bring us not only pleasure, but insight.

Why aren't we spending our small moments of free time doing things that will enrich us? The things that so many of us have craved to do all our lives? Why aren't we stimulating our brains and making our lives fuller?

It takes some time and takes some effort, but no matter how exhausted we are after our long and stressful days, the way to break ourselves out of the stress-inducing trap of mindless time-wasting is to think of all the amazing and en-

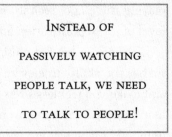

INSTEAD OF

PASSIVELY WATCHING

PEOPLE TALK, WE NEED

TO TALK TO PEOPLE!

riching options that are right under our noses.

All of us have passions, interests, hobbies—things that help us appreciate the quality of life. Whenever you feel yourself getting seduced by the pleasure of mindlessness, think of something that will make you resonate with the energy of life, that will *zap* you with excitement and vigor.

MUSIC is the thing that does it for most people. Not only is music transformative—with the power to take you away to a different psychological state—scientists have determined that indeed music has a powerful effect on the brain. Listening to certain types of music are even believed to increase certain brain functions (the "Mozart Effect") and have calming and/or stimulating effects on the neurons of the brain. Some scientists believe that simply being exposed to music will increase a child's creativity and ability to learn.

Listen to music, or even better, play music. Practice a musical instrument, or sing! Participating in music provides amazing stimulation for the brain; it helps certain sorts of cognitive learning, and it's fun. People in our grandparents' generation always had live music around the house: people playing the piano, recitals, people singing. It elevated the level of joy, sophistication and community in their lives.

Whatever kind of music you enjoy, it's clear that music has the ability to elevate your mood, calm your nerves, and make you feel less stress and more pleasure. Music can help you experience that wondrous feeling that life is worth living, that genius is around you, that there is amazing talent and passion in the world—and you're a part of it.

LITERATURE. Since you're actually reading these words in a book, I'm probably preaching to the converted here, but bear with me.

We have understood for centuries that reading is the best way that mankind has for enriching itself. It's the best way for information to be passed among human beings in a way that is intense, stimulating, enriching, and nourishing. Not to mention that books can be an awful lot of fun.

I can never understand why people choose to waste time when they can be reading instead. Even if their interests don't lie in fine literature, it's a whole lot more stimulating to the brain and nurturing to the soul to simply read. Whether it's a mystery novel, a romance, a biography of a movie star, or a book of non-fiction on a subject of interest, the brain gets more information, more stimulation, and more exercise by reading a book than by watching something unengaging on television.

Try picking up a book for half an hour the next time you're tempted by television. Your body and your brain will appreciate it.

THE INTERNET. We now live in the most amazing time ever on the planet when it comes to ways to keep ourselves entertained and informed. And to my mind one of the most incredible innovations is the Internet.

Imagine! Instead of spending half an hour watching two jerks beating each other up on *Jerry Springer,* you could be online, investigating any subject in the world that interests you, no matter how obscure or how popular.

There are websites devoted to virtually everything in the world. You can look up the work of practically any author, musician, artist, scientist, professional wrestler, architect, race-car driver, film director, anything! Whatever your passion is, you can get on the Internet and surf away for hours, finding sites, articles, and links devoted to the thing that turns you on.

The Internet now gives everyone the opportunity to dive into their obsessions and discover the depths of their excitement. Are you someone who grew up wondering about life on other planets? About who had the best hitting average against left-handed pitchers? About the lives of Elizabethan poets? About the structure of the world's tallest buildings?

It used to be that you'd have to spend days in libraries, searching out books and magazines, trying to pursue the details of your interest. Now, you turn on your computer, get on line, and start looking around. Isn't that wonderful?

And not only that, the Internet gives you the ability to communicate with people who share your passions, and that's something revolutionary. Where you used to be the only one in your town checking out books from the library on Flamenco dancing (or even if you weren't, you had no way of knowing who took the book out when you brought it back), now you can go online, find fan sites, join a chat group or a club, and have a virtual talk with people who share your interests all over the world.

If you ask me, there are few better ways to spend a spare hour or so than to dive into the Internet and pursue a subject that inspires you and read everything you can, no matter how obscure. It helps to reinforce for you the very important inner understanding that 1) you are a person of deep interests and enthusiasms; 2) you're connected to a community that feels the same passions you do; 3) the world is a place where the things you love can thrive; and 4) that you're capable of learning and growing.

These are the emotions that keep us alive and buzzing instead of deadly and bored.

BOOK GROUPS. Despite my enthusiasm for the Internet, there's one thing profoundly missing from an online experience. Real, living and breathing people. As engaged as you can get by sharing your passion with someone in cyberspace, it's a second-rate stand-in for sharing your passion with someone in person.

Which is why I think that the current explosion in book discussion groups is just a sensational way to spend some free time. Not only do you get to read fine books, which is itself an enriching experience, you then get to have real intimate and intense conversation with other intelligent people about what you've just read. You share ideas and enthusiasms and can mutually excite one another into seeing things in a new way.

Most book groups meet once a month, though some meet once a week. Some book lovers join more than one group, maybe one that reads contemporary fiction and one that reads biographies. Every town these days has book discussion groups that can usually be found by asking at a local bookstore or library, or by checking town listings in a local paper. If you have trouble finding one that feels right, start your own with a handful of friends!

INSPIRING VIDEO. For most of us, our television watching is no longer limited to the schedules of the three major networks. When we feel like watching television, we have so much choice and so many options, we need to go toward things that will make us feel inspired instead of insipid.

Why would anyone watch Geraldo Rivera talking about OJ Simpson for the third year running when we could be watching an interesting, innovative movie on a cable channel? Or learning something about nature on the Discovery Channel? Or learning how to cook a sensational meal on the Food Network? Or listening to an inspiring lecture (by someone like me!) on PBS? Or being inspired by an athletic performance on ESPN?

When our grandparents watched television, they were watching inspirational programming: there was live theater

> ### The Tombstone
> ### No One Wants #4:
>
> HERE LIES JANE DOE,
> 1955–2009. SHE COULD
> HAVE HAD TWO MORE FULL
> WAKING YEARS IF NOT FOR
> WATCHING *Jerry Springer*
> AND *"Who Wants to Be*
> *a Millionaire?"*

broadcast by playwrights like Paddy Chayefsky and Tennessee Williams. There was innovative comedy by people like Elaine May. There was suspense by masters like Alfred Hitchcock. We need to pick programs that re-create the intelligence of that era.

And if there really is nothing on your five-hundred channel television system that turns you on, plug in a video tape and watch *Citizen Kane* again, or a production of *The Marriage of Figaro*, or a documentary about the first moon landing.

The real point of all of this is: you have the power of choice. I still can't believe that 23 million people chose to watch those idiots get married, and that scares me a little. It scares me because I *know* that if they were given better options, if they weren't the targets of relentless promotion tactics, and if they weren't so burned-out from the stresses that society places on all of us today, people would be making different choices.

I am saddened by the thought that so many of us are so overwhelmed by the stresses of life that we choose mindlessness over enrichment. And I am even more saddened that corporations have encouraged the phenomenon because it's an easier way to make money.

But I'm also excited to see the rise of media and phenomenon that shows that growing numbers of people are finding mindlessness unacceptable. We're surfing the Internet. We're joining book groups. We're watching alternative programming on cable and on video. We're going to the theater.

The human spirit needs growth and stimulation, and despite the best efforts of some factions of society to seduce it with mindlessness, many many people are using the power of their spirit and ingenuity to fight back.

Why not join them?

Take a Socrates Break.
Don't ask me, ask yourself:

❖ *How often do you watch television to "waste time" rather than because you are really interested in the program offered?*

❖ *Do you sometimes feel yourself getting more emotionally engaged with the "celebrities" you watch on TV than with people in your own life?*

❖ *Think of a time in which you felt insulted because a television program was mindless or dumb. Did you switch it off in protest, or did you continue to watch nevertheless?*

❖ When was the last time you read a book for the pure pleasure of it, not for work or self-improvement?

❖ Do you find yourself discussing television shows with people instead of discussing what's happening in your own life?

❖ Do you sometimes find yourself watching one TV show after another, without even necessarily caring what is coming on next?

❖ Does it anger you that a "celebrity" like Darva Conger gets paid fortunes of money for no apparent talent, skill or contribution to society? If not, why not?

❖ The average teenager watches 1100 hours of television a year: that's almost an entire month of time. If you were given that much free time in one lump, starting now, how would you spend it?

❖ Is there a television show you feel you "can't miss"—so much so that real life events, like a dinner party invitation, feel like an intrusion? Does that make sense?

❖ Think of your favorite television show. Does it truly engage and entertain you? Now think of some of the other shows you watch. Do they engage you the same way? If not, why do you watch them?

5

A Three-Dollar Glass of Water

On consumerism and sanity

THIS MORNING I DID SOMETHING that many people I know would be shocked to find out about. But I just couldn't help myself. I gave in. It was risky, I know. It was daring, taboo. But what can I say? I like to live on the edge.

I took a glass, opened my faucet, filled it with tap water, and, yes, I recklessly and with wild abandon, drank it.

And lived to tell the tale.

What is with people these days and water?
People are fixated with drinking expensive bottled water. "Oh, is that Evian you're drinking? Or is it Poland Spring? San Pellegrino?" "No, no, I prefer Nepi." "I only drink Perrier from the coast of France." "Oh, I drink Calistoga from

California." "I only drink water from the artesian wells in Fiji."

I once overheard someone in a restaurant complain to a waiter that the bottled water he served her was "too rich."

Are we insane? Or just waterlogged?

Why do we feel more protected drinking water out of a pretty blue-tinged bottle called Botswana Mineral Springs than from our town water supply? It's ironic and true that many of these waters come from foreign countries where the government bottling regulations are virtually nonexistent.

We pay good money to buy water from France, where pigs are walking around peeing in the fields, but we won't drink the water that is monitored for purity by our own community. We fork over three bucks or more for something that might be polluted, when we could be drinking something that is tested to be safe, for free. Can you spell D—U—H?

The reason we all do it, of course, is that it's "in" to drink bottled water.

Have you noticed that everyone carries bottles of water with them wherever they go? They have little holders with straps to carry the bottles around in; straps that, of course, leave the labels plainly visible.

Listen, I have nothing against drinking water. I understand and appreciate that it's very important for people to stay well-hydrated. But unless you're trekking across the Himalayas, you're probably never far enough from a source of water that you have to carry your own supply everywhere you go.

But of course, that's not the real issue. The issue is this: people want to show off what kind of water they drink the same way they show off what label of clothing they wear. Water has become status. Schlepping around a quart of water tells people that

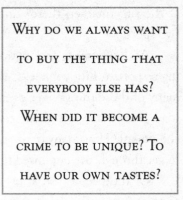

WHY DO WE ALWAYS WANT TO BUY THE THING THAT EVERYBODY ELSE HAS? WHEN DID IT BECOME A CRIME TO BE UNIQUE? TO HAVE OUR OWN TASTES?

you're not some shlub that drinks from the tap. It shows that 1) you are healthy and 2) you are well-off and 3) you have better taste than the riffraff that drinks water for free.

The overwhelming trend to drink bottled water says a lot about our society today, and I think that what it says is disturbing.

As far as consumerism is concerned, we're more and more becoming a society of lemmings. I find it astounding, but it's true. It's another very clear manifestation of our damaging cultural tendency to want to fit into the crowd rather than stand out from it.

I see it in my own town. It's the weirdest thing. All of a sudden, everywhere I turn, somebody is driving a truck. Not a sport utility vehicle (which I'll get to in a moment), but a truck! It's amazing. Women, men, everybody's driving a truck. I wondered if all of a sudden there was a boom in the construction business. But, no. It just became the "in" thing to drive.

So every time I try to pull my car into a parking spot

at the supermarket, there's another damn truck taking up two spots.

And, of course, on a national level, everybody is driving a sports utility vehicle. Can anyone tell me why? How many of those things have ever really had to go off a paved road? How many of them cart around massive sporting equipment? How many of them need their four-wheel drive to get through the unplowed tundra?

Of the people you know that drive them, does even one person use the damn thing to go rough-riding through the woods in a blinding snowstorm? Does anybody strap surfboards to the roof and boogie across the sand? In fact, does anybody really use them for anything other than regular suburban trips to the mall and to the dentist and to the office park and back? Of course not.

But that doesn't matter. We've all become the target of a multimillion-dollar promotion campaign to convince us that an SUV is the "cool" thing to drive. Those campaigns are so persuasive and provocative that they are nearly impossible to avoid and to ignore. So everybody is paying an extra $15,000 or so (not to mention probably getting about ten miles less to the gallon of gas, doubling their insurance bill, and contributing more than their share to the pollution of the environment) in order to drive around in this thing that's really nothing more than a station wagon on stilts.

You gotta hand it to Detroit. They took what we used to think of as something a little boring, a family utility vehicle (i.e.: a station wagon), raised it a few inches off the ground, gave it a fancy outdoorsy name like "Himalaya" and called it a "sports utility vehicle." Now when we get behind the wheel of what is basically the same damn car, instead of feeling like an old fart with three kids in the back, we feel like we're a fearless sportsman on our way to the Australian Outback.

It's sad but true, many people in our culture allow their products to define who they are. But of course they would; for decades now, we've been the target of these massive advertising, promotion and marketing campaigns that have tried desperately to convince us of just that: that by buying a particular product, you can live a fantasy. And if you buy the luxurious brand, you've proven that you belong with the "in crowd."

According to James Twitchell, author of *Lead Us Into Temptation: the Triumph of American Materialism*, "luxury marketing has been exceedingly good at repackaging basic products as items of desire. It's as simple a thing as Evian water and as complicated as a Lincoln Town Car," says Twitchell. "Advertising media generate luxury value where our rational minds tell us no such value exists. Evian is bottled water. What's being marketed here is non-intrinsic value."

You see this phenomenon everywhere. People seem obsessed with buying ostentatious things that show off just how much status and money they have. I was shopping for a baby gift last week, and I was appalled by some of the things I saw for sale in the infant section of a major national department store.

The crib that was most prominently displayed—and

the one that I saw several sets of parents ogling—was a giant castle-shaped structure that looked Napoleonic: great iron pillars holding up each corner, with big plumes at the tops. It didn't look like a crib, it looked like the set for a new production of Shakespeare's *Macbeth*. It was priced at $1200.

I saw someone buying a gold leaf bassinette. I saw people buying cashmere baby blankets. And, of course, the only real quandary for many of the people shopping that day was whether to buy the Ralph Lauren or the Tommy Hilfiger diapers.

Pardon me, but does this make any sense whatsoever? I love babies, don't get me wrong. I had three of my own and I have ten grandchildren that I'm nuts about. But a baby doesn't know where it is, as long as it's kept safe and comfortable. Put it in a soft blanket, and it doesn't make a damn bit of difference if its crib is lined with gold leaf or polyester.

Let's face it, the baby doesn't know if the mobile hanging over its crib came from Kmart or from Brookstone. It doesn't matter if the blanket on the crib is made of cotton or of chinchilla. The only thing a baby needs is love, attention, stimulation and human contact. But what they're getting is top-of-the-line merchandise.

Like virtually every society in the world, ours is one that is obsessed with status. But in most societies, status is achieved by class, or by a strict caste system. Here it's not so clear, and the easiest way for us to show our status and good taste is to blatantly purchase and show off the consumer goods that demonstrate status and good taste. In an ancient tribe, you might have achieved status if you lived near the Serengeti. Here, you get it by buying a jeep named Serengeti.

We get our signals about which consumer goods grant status from the media, which is, of course, run by advertising dollars from big corporations that want us to buy their expensive merchandise. So the next thing we know, we're all driving SUVs, drinking bottled water, and wearing Tommy Hilfiger blue jeans. It doesn't matter that these things cost twice as much as an alternative that might even be of a better quality. Having the media-approved upscale item makes a statement about who we are, and that's very important to most people.

Now people are eating protein bars as snacks. Have you seen these? Peanut butter and chocolate "power bars." Who are they kidding? It's a Reese's peanut butter cup with a little whole wheat and some vitamins in the middle! They're something like five hundred calories, but people eat them for the supplements with the same self-righteousness that they take their vitamins in the morning. It's for good health!

I swear, if anybody could tell the difference between a "protein bar" and what my kids used to think was a candy bar, I'll eat my peanut butter and chocolate-flavored hat!

But the way the product is marketed makes us feel

good about ourselves. Eat a candy bar while you're walking home from work, you're a fat pig. But eat a power bar while you're walking home from work, you're an athlete. What's that say about our society's ability to think for itself and use its own common sense?

It clearly shows a lack of common sense. But we're not stupid people. What is it that we're searching for?

There's a lot that we get from consumerism. We get nurtured; we get instant satisfaction; we feel validated. And perhaps most important these days, we feel comfort. We're all so in-need of something to make us feel cared for and understood that we go searching for it in the temples that society has built for us: the shopping mall.

A good example of this: have you noticed that these days everything we look at is sold and marketed specifically to reduce stress?

Once, stress was perceived as pandemic, then marketers came out of the woodwork with products and services. You can buy creams that reduce stress in your face, oils you put in your bathwaters, tapes with special sounds, clothing that has been blessed by monks who are themselves totally relaxed. Even dogs and cats have been targeted. You can actually put your pet into analysis to calm their behavior.

There's aromatherapy. Lavender Oil reduces stress. You buy a ring and put it on your lamp, and it releases a fragrance that permeates your room and is supposed to have a calming effect and help you sleep.

Everybody lights candles. Soften the lights, draw the shades. Light up one of those huge scented candles and feel the anxieties of the day float away (that is, until your house goes up in flames: USA *Today* reports that there are 30 percent more house fires in the last ten years because more people burn candles).

People buy pillows that have corn or something inside of them that are supposed to reduce stress. My question is: how can I sleep if I'm worried that tossing and turning will turn my pillow into polenta?

There are lines of shoes to reduce stress.

There are lightbulbs to reduce stress.

There are restaurants specifically pitched as selling "comfort foods": foods that remind us of what our mothers fed us when we were young (mashed potatoes, rice pudding, meat loaf).

A few years ago I noticed that fine upscale stores started selling zen fountains, which were made out of carved stone and were quite lovely works of art. People believe that these zen fountains help calm nerves and reduce stress through the gentle sound of water running over rocks.

Today they're being mass produced and sold at discount stores. Not that I have anything against discount stores, it's the marketing of zen serenity as another consumer product that I think is absurd. Everybody buys zen fountains but nobody has the time to go listen to the actual sound of water running over rocks in a brook.

Want a cup of tea before bed? No, no. Can't have tea.

You've got to have a "soothing" herbal tea. Look at the names of those Celestial Seasonings teas. Tension Tamer Tea, Grandma's Tummy Mint Tea, Sleepytime. I fall asleep just reading the names.

There are exotic skin care lines that are sold in stores with smoked glass and candles and polished wood where everything smells like apples. They are marketing nature. Every product has some strange name with the word "root" or "rock" or "essence" in it.

Now some of these things may actually be effective in reducing stress. Aromatherapy, for example, has been found to have benefits. And, certainly, massage and relaxation techniques are effective. But the answer to the inner chaos that so many of us feel cannot be purchased. Buying a zen fountain over the Internet won't get you very far. Serenity must be produced from within. My grandmother found peace in saying the Rosary. She said it every day, without fail. As a young woman I would often ask her, "What do you pray for?" and the answer was always the same. "I pray for a peaceful life for myself and others, and a happy death."

I remember admonishing her to stop thinking about death. It is only in the last few years that I realize how wise she was about life and death. Her life's purpose was about reaching a life of harmony and spirituality. Isn't that what we're all looking for?

And you know what? Her wish was granted. She died at ninety-seven on Valentine's Day with a smile on her face, surrounded by the people she loved.

———

We shop because it makes us feel good. It makes us feel cared for; in these days when we're all so overworked and overstressed, if there's no one at home to tell us that we look good and that they love us, well, there's always Banana Republic and the Body Shop. When

> OUR GRANDPARENTS DIDN'T SHOP TILL THEY DROPPED. THEY BOUGHT WHAT THEY NEEDED FOR THE DAY, AND DIDN'T SPEND MORE THAN THEY HAD IN THEIR POCKET.

we come home we can take a hot soothing bath and put on a new silk robe, and for those lovely moments, we feel cared for.

The preoccupation we all seem to have with shopping is a sick thing. "Shop Till You Drop." What the hell is that? Can you imagine? Now, I know that people use that phrase with their tongue-in-cheek, but still, come on. There's something to it. People use the phrase jokingly, but it's only funny because there's a ring of truth to it. Going to spend a day at the shopping mall, walking and schlepping around for hours, is a perfectly normal and acceptable way of spending time. People say "I'm going to shop till I drop," but they never say "I'm going to pray until I faint" or "I'm going to kiss my child until I pass out."

Isn't that a little wacky?

But, since for many of us shopping is a form of nourishment, we take what we can get. It makes us feel good; it makes us feel like we've done something to make our lives better. It helps us enhance our self-image—after all, we've just spent a lot of money to buy something that will improve our lives or our looks. Why shouldn't we feel good about that?

And, let's face it, buying new things is pleasurable. You see the way children's faces light up when they're given a new toy; it's completely natural. Acquiring new things stimulates the pleasure center in our brains, and that pleasure center is insatiable. Buy the child one new toy and he or she wants more and more and more. We become hooked on feeling the pleasure of acquisition, and often that is the reason we buy things, not for the legitimate reason of satisfying a need for the new item itself.

I've fallen into this trap myself. Listen, for many years now, I've been keeping a quite harried and difficult schedule, like most Americans. I'm on the road at least four or five days a week, sometimes even more; I'm writing books and articles; I'm taping my annual show for PBS; I make publicity appearances to support those projects. When I get home, I'm lucky if I get to say hello to my husband, much less have any real bonding time with him. I also crave seeing my kids and my grandchildren, and it's so hard to fit that all in.

Around four years ago, I realized that when I'd get home on a weekend, I found myself spending way too much time buying clothes. I'd go to a local shop that I like, and I'd buy three or four tops, three or four pairs of pants. All nice stuff, all clothes I'd be proud to wear.

And I'd get home and hang these things in the closet,

and often they'd just sit there. I was happy to have them; someday maybe I'd actually wear them.

But the truth was, I didn't *need* those clothes. What I needed was more time with my family, and more nurturing. But because I didn't have that, I was giving myself something else to make me feel good. I was feeding the pleasure center.

What's wrong with that? Well, it leaves you feeling even more bereft in the long run, because you're not getting the thing you really crave. And on top of that, you're broke.

It seems to me that the most important thing to understand to make shopping a truly nurturing and sane experience is the difference between buying because it feels good, and buying what we need.

I think again about our grandparents' generation, and the difference between how they consumed and how we do.

When our grandparents went shopping, they had saved up for the thing that they wanted. Money was scarcer for most people, and therefore more important. Purchases were made in the spirit of *seriousness*. They waited months before making any major purchase, and sometimes even any minor purchase. They'd ruminate: Do we really need this? What else will we do without if we buy it? Will we regret this the next time our rent is due?

People in our grandparents' generation didn't have credit cards—and I think that one single invention of the twentieth century has put more stress and insanity into people's lives than just about any other. These days, how often do people think about *need* when they go shopping? The spending of money is now a sporting event. We buy now, and worry about it a couple of months later when the credit card bills come due. We have to feed the pleasure center.

It's as if we fill the void from other areas of life with all the crap that we put on our credit cards. So many of us feel unfulfilled in our work, in our familial relationships; we feel so stressed from all the other pressures of life that I've talked about throughout this book, that we feel "hey, I deserve it. If I want that little silk jacket, why shouldn't I have it?" And when we can put it on our credit card and take it home that very minute without the pain of actually earning and saving the money that it takes to buy it, sure, for a while, it feels great. But ultimately, it harms us both psychologically and financially.

The sorts of pleasure our grandparents got from having people over to the house, from savoring food and conversation and the arts, we often get from buying new stuff. Let's face it, who could blame us? Most pleasures in today's world come with warnings from the surgeon general. Shopping is not one of them.

But like virtually everything else in our society today, I fear that what used to be a pleasurable experience has become one fraught with peril. If you're not conscious of the peril, consumerism can make your life very unpleasant.

Stay alert to the following:

The Corporate Marketplace vs. The Human Marketplace

One of the great pleasures of shopping, it seems to me, should be that it enhances your vision of what the world has to offer. There's a wonderful diversity out there in the world, and a lot of differing tastes and styles and smells and crafts.

The marketplace is a wonderful thing. Listen, in its most basic and nurturing form, the market is a place where people in the community gather to exchange their goods and services. Still, even these days, go to a true rural community and there is probably, at least once a week, a local marketplace where farmers, craftsmen and artisans come and sell their wares. Shopping there is a lovely and almost spiritual experience. It's about human connection, and products that were created with care. Entire families often come and participate in selling their wares. People walk around and make real human contact. They taste and smell and touch. They say hello to the person who grew the corn, or churned the butter, or painted the mug.

It's so rare, these days, for most of us to really feel the connection of the human marketplace. For me, the thing that is most enriching and enhancing about shopping is finding something fresh, and meeting people along the way. I go out of my way to find stores where someone is actually involved in the products they sell: some little craft shop where the artist's workbench is in the back; a clothes store where there is a unique sensibility behind the selection of clothes—and where someone can really help me figure out what might look good around these hips.

Shopping should make you feel good about the thing you buy, and the people you buy it from. It's great to go into the marketplace and see things that carry the stamp of people's workmanship and selection. It's fun to go to stores that have a personality.

But so much of shopping has become a corporate experience, not a human one.

We go to these stores that look exactly the same, no matter where we live. These days, whether you're walking down the main street of a small town, or Fifth Avenue in New York, or some marbleized shopping mall out in the 'burbs, all the stores are the same. You've got a Gap (or two), a Williams Sonoma, a Banana Republic, a Barnes and Noble, a Starbucks, a Disney Store, a Body Shop, and a J. Crew. If you're dropped blindfolded into the shopping district of some town, you'll have no idea if you're in Cedar Rapids, Iowa, or Austin, Texas.

There's something awfully boring about that, don't you think? That we all shop in the same twelve stores? Isn't it a little limiting, and therefore dispiriting, to think that we have so few options? That the only colors that we can feel comfortable wearing in a given season are the ones featured by the Gap and its subsidiaries?

Keep in mind that the human marketplace can nurture your soul while the corporate one tries to exploit it. It's a trap you don't have to fall into. Go out of your way to find the stores and the markets that carry the personality of a human being. Talk to the shopkeepers. Make it an opportunity to connect, not simply an opportunity to consume.

And you can do the same thing if you shop in a big corporate store. Listen, I don't suggest that you can't have a good experience shopping at major retailers. I like the clothes at several major stores, and, indeed, you can buy this book at chain bookstores—God bless them.

But keep your head about you. Remember that these stores exist to serve you and give you what you want. If you like their merchandise, enjoy them. But don't get drawn into the trap of shopping there just because everyone else does. If you spend your life trying to do what everyone else does, you're going to be a mighty unhappy, boring person.

Consuming Kids

Remember a few Christmases ago, when it seemed like every parent in the Northern Hemisphere was trying to find a Tickle Me Elmo doll? It was incredible: lines would form around the block at the mere rumor that a truck was heading in the direction of a toy store. People were running ads in newspapers (this was before eBay!) and offering to sell their toys at fifteen or twenty times face value—and bidding wars would ensue! Fist fights were breaking out when parents were scrambling over the opening of new inventory.

Now, of course there's one way of looking at this phenomenon that is positive and uplifting: look at how hard so many parents want to please their children.

But think for a minute about the message that this

kind of behavior sends to the kids. Inappropriate acts and fighting aside, the frenzy to fulfill the desire for a mass-produced toy is sending a terrible signal. It's like telling the kids, "I'll do everything I can to get this toy for you, because I know you'll be miserable without it."

Buying into this kind of frenzy validates the worst impulses of consumerism. It sends the signal to kids that you agree with the way they're feeling: that the acquisition of a particular product that they saw on TV is tantamount to their happiness.

We have to do everything we can to stop passing this craziness on to our kids. We need to make them see that the stuff that is advertised to them on Saturday morning television has nothing to do with their happiness. We have to give them the wherewithal to entertain themselves rather than give in to their cravings for merchandise.

In our grandparents' generation, kids weren't the targets of marketing. It was easier for parents then. They were able to teach this lesson without the disappointment that comes along with kids seeing the object of their desire constantly paraded in front of them. It's much harder now, but it's a challenge for modern parents that cannot be overlooked.

We have to teach children how to separate the feelings of "wanting" what they see on television from the reality of real life. I know parents who actively make fun of commercials with their kids and teach them what it is that they're watching. They say things like "wow, look at that stupid toy that they're trying to get you to want. It's ugly and probably will fall apart as soon as you get it home." Or things like "that cereal may look good on TV and they tell you it's delicious because they want you to buy it. But it's really very unhealthy for kids and I will never bring it into this house."

It works sometimes. Of course, it doesn't work all the time. Kids want a lot of what they see. But inappropriately giving in to their desires will only make them grow into the sorts of adults who are the biggest victims of corporate marketers: those who feel they can't be happy unless they buy everything they want.

After all, what will happen if a kid doesn't get the toy that he's craving on a particular birthday or holiday? Will he jump out a window? Will he shoot himself? Will he hate his parents forever?

No, five minutes later he'll move on to something else and will have learned the lesson that he can live without a Tickle Me Elmo doll.

It's Pokemon he can't live without.

Today's Styles

My grandmother used to shop for clothes, of course, like everyone. But her closet was spare. She had an intrinsic sense of what looked good on her.

I never heard my grandmother say anything remotely like "God, I've got to get myself a pair of those new Capri pants!"

In their generation, people went out to buy things that they needed. They weren't pressured by modern marketing techniques to always desire something new and different.

We, on the other hand, are bombarded every waking moment (and, lets face it, probably in our dreams, too) with images of what's new in the stores. Whether it's capri pants, or the new Mercedes sports utility vehicle, or Calvin Klein's "Obsession," or a new album by Madonna—we're constantly enticed to *want*. Every time we turn around, sometimes without even knowing it, we're being seduced into wanting something else.

And why not? These products are often things that look good, or sound good, or smell good or taste good. Of course we'd want them. On a major level: if you look at an ad for a new Jaguar convertible, of course it's going to be enticing. Who wouldn't want to own such a sleek and magnificent vehicle? Not to mention, who wouldn't like to feel the status that comes along with driving it? But then again, it's not an option for most of us. Who has seventy thousand dollars to spare?

That's an easy choice. We can't have it. But we know it's out there and that makes us feel bad.

But on a more minor level: we can all afford a new sweater from the Gap. And the ads make them look good. Of course we want one. And that's something we can afford!

Of course, there are fifty other things we've been seduced into wanting as well, and if we bought them all we'd max out our credit cards. So we wouldn't feel good for long.

We have to stay conscious and be vigilant about understanding the difference between the things we **really** want and the things we need from the things we have been brainwashed into wanting.

If you feel yourself lusting after some newly promoted product, and thinking "I've got to have those; I don't know what I'll do if I don't have one of those . . ." you're probably in trouble. What's the source of the craving? Why do you want it so badly? Can you wait six months before you buy it? After all, if it's so wonderful, you'll still want it then.

If you want something way too much, you're expecting that outside product to fill some inner void. It's the wrong place to look.

You have to peruse advertising with a sense of irony and distance. *What kind of crap are they trying to sell me now?* You have to think through every purchase with the wisdom of Moses. Don't feel pressured to buy the style of the season just to fit in.

The Bargain Trap

How many times have you heard someone say "I just found this amazing silk jacket. It was only ninety-five dollars. I saw it last week for three hundred dollars. What a deal!"

Now, let's be real here. Is anyone naive enough to believe that that jacket was ever really worth three hundred dollars? No, it's probably worth about fifty dollars, and was insanely overpriced before. Now it's only mildly overpriced but we feel like we've saved money when what we've really done is buy another thing we probably don't need.

How many times have you heard "You can't have too many black pants . . ."? Oh yeah? Who says? When will you know that you have too many black pants? When God speaks to you and throws lightning bolts into your closet? When they come bursting out of your closet of their own free will?

Of course you can have too many black pants, if you're buying them on credit cards, and you're giving up other things that can enrich your soul. If you ever have had the thought "you just can't have too many of . . ." whatever it is you like, then shopping just might be an addiction for you.

I hear friends say: "I found a bag at Marshall's for twenty dollars that I saw three weeks ago at Neiman Marcus for fifty! It took three hours of looking around, but I found something great!"

Is that really a good way to spend a day?

Here's something that is simply beyond me: virtually all over the country now, and certainly within a few hours distance from every major city, there is a massive outlet mall development. The fantasy presented when these things were first created was that this was where you could get the stuff from the major manufacturers that were either remainders or irregulars—but at rock-bottom prices. Now, of course, we all know that these stores carry virtually the same merchandise as any other of the non "factory outlet"

PEOPLE MAKE PILGRIMAGES TO THESE OUTLET MALLS. THEY ARE THE "LOURDES" OF MODERN SOCIETY!

stores, but usually with a limited selection and still at somewhat lower prices. And people travel, sometimes several hours, to shop at these stores. Hotels spring up around them for the people who want to make a weekend out of it. Local bus companies arrange tours, and lines form around the block with people heading to spend a day of their lives at the outlet shops.

Now, is it me? This is a truly amazing phenomenon. People spending hours, if not days, traveling to a huge overcrowded development where they can rummage through the baseball fields worth of stuff, looking for the diamond in the haystack.

Yet, people love it! "I found a suit for two hundred dollars that retails for five hundred!" Well, yeah: but you spent three days finding it. How much is your time worth to you?

Now don't get me wrong, I've got nothing against getting a good bargain. Anyone who pays full price for everything is just plain stupid. But my problem is with our tendency to buy stuff we don't need just because it looks like a bargain.

Is searching for bargain merchandise really a worthwhile way to spend days of our time? Is there anything about shopping for bargains that is going to nurture you? That's going to enrich you? That's going to feed your soul or make you a happier person?

What will no doubt happen, because it happens to all of us, is that you're going to buy a bunch of crap that you don't need. Then you'll get the credit card bill and you'll lament having spent that money, and then a year later you'll forget everything you bought and throw it all out when it's time to "simplify your life."

Maybe the nurturing thing would be to take the money you were going to use to buy shoes, and instead buy a pair of shoes for someone who can't afford them. Or to take the time you were going to spend waiting on line to get your daughter another Beanie Baby, or an electronic barking dog, or whatever the must-have toy is for this holiday season, and instead take her out to the playground to play catch, or take her to lunch and have a conversation with her, or write a poem together.

Be an active role model for kids. Communication and shared activity is far superior to something from a toy superstore. Of course that's going to take a lot of convincing, and a few tears. But, in the long run, you'll be there with them when the Pokemon character is long forgotten.

⮾

We all need to remain constantly aware of the fact that we are the targets of seduction. And the techniques are sophisticated—it's not just TV commercials and ads in newspapers—it's all around us, in every image that is presented by the media and the advertising community. Wherever we turn, there is some image that is designed to make us *want* something.

The best way to help yourself is to replace the need to buy with the need to feed your soul. Think about the things that really nurture you: things that engage your brain, that fill your spirit, that enrich your life. There are so many ways to spend time that can make us truly richer and more fulfilled as human beings.

> ## The Tombstone No One Wants #5
>
> HERE LIES JANE DOE.
> IN HER CLOSET ARE
> SEVENTY-FIVE BLOUSES
> AND TEN LITTLE BLACK
> DRESSES. SHE HARDLY HAD
> TIME TO WEAR THEM.

The next time you think of taking a day trip to the outlet mall, think of all the things you can do instead. How about a day trip to a museum? When was the last time you took a day and really pursued a passion or a hobby? Think of how much better it will make you feel to spend a day doing something to enrich your soul, or demonstrate the incredible ability of the human spirit, rather than doing something to enrich a national retail chain.

Look inside yourself and think of the things that really turn you on, that make you tingle with the realization that life is fantastic! It's different for everybody, but there are so many ways to spend a day that can make you feel in-sync with the amazing possibilities of the human spirit:

❖ THEATRE. For many people, going to see a live theatrical performance is energizing, elevating, and wondrous. There's something about the communal nature of the experience that makes it feel fuller and more ritualistic than other forms of literature, and the live actors give you a feeling of connection. They feed your imagination.

❖ SPORT. Going to see a live sporting event is, for many people, the most exciting, powerful and energizing way to spend time. It gives you an appreciation of the wonder of the human body, and the power of the human will. A major sporting event, like an Olympic competition, also creates enormous feelings of community involvement and spirit.

❖ ARCHITECTURE. For some people, going to see a magnificent building, or a bridge, or a skyscraper, can incite amazing feelings of wonder and passion— helping us again to see the amazing potential of the human species.

❖ ANIMALS. Have you ever stood close to a giraffe? Have you ever looked right into his eyes with those huge eyelashes, and have him stare back? It's such a powerful and wondrous experience. Animals of all sorts teach us so much about the ways in which we are unique on the planet, and the ways in which we are just a part of the ecosystem. A personal interaction with a live animal can be a transformative experience.

❖ CLASSES. In every community there are resources that you can take advantage of, if you do a little research. Most local colleges offer classes to the community, either as part of adult learning programs or as programs to audit their accredited courses. How much better would it make you feel to spend an hour a week learning something you've always dreamed of, instead of buying another blouse at Neiman Marcus? Take a life drawing class. Learn to play a musical instrument. Study poetry (either reading it, or writing it). Learn how a computer works. The possibilities are endless. You can even take courses on the Internet!

The possibilities for all of us are endless, as soon as we make the conscious decision to do things that will enrich us as human beings.

When I think of the pressures of consumerism, I think of an elderly aunt of mine who is ill and housebound, who stays at home and watches those TV shopping channels day in and day out. I swear, she is quickly going through her bank account buying stuff she is never going to use. She buys little trinkets to beautify the house, new small appliances that I doubt she'll ever use (she doesn't cook gourmet meals, why does she need a set of twenty-two Japanese knives?). She buys lovely pieces of jewelry she sees on the show, but she never dresses up to go out!

She is clearly living out a fantasy, one in which the sad things in her life are forgotten about in the pleasure of opening boxes full of pretty new merchandise. That pleasure center in her brain keeps wanting more and more, and cubic zirconium necklaces clearly fill the bill!

Luckily, she has enough money so that she won't end

up on the street because of this habit, and in the last days of her life, who wants to take this pleasure away from her? So she continues to sit there with her remote control and her telephone at the ready, looking for something good that she can buy.

But for me, she is symbolic of everything that is wrong with the way we buy today. She is a victim of our consumer culture, sitting on her deathbed hoping for redemption and pleasure through the things that she buys.

I don't know about you, but I'm damned sure that I don't want to spend my last days like that!

Take a Socrates Break.
Don't ask me, ask yourself:

- ❖ *Do you go shopping for the pure pleasure of the act, without an actual need for something?*

- ❖ *Look through your closets: do you actually wear the clothes you have there? Do you need any more?*

- ❖ *When choosing between two brands, do you buy the more expensive without really knowing if it's superior?*

- ❖ *Do you buy the less expensive one without really knowing if it is of such poor quality as to be useless in the long run?*

- ❖ *Are you seduced into buying something because it's a bargain, even if you don't need it?*

❖ *How would you feel if you drove up to an event in your beloved Ford Taurus station wagon, and everyone else was driving a foreign-made sports utility vehicle?*

❖ *How often do you make sure that you actually have the money to pay for an item before you charge it to a credit card?*

❖ *When visiting a new city or town, do you like to shop in stores that are funky and unique, or chain stores that are familiar to you from home?*

❖ *Do you search the bargain tables incessantly? Just what do you think you're going to find there, and is it really worth the time?*

❖ *Can you ever remember feeling that you were just going to die if you didn't get some new product? Now stop and think about it. What, really, was so important?*

6

Just Have Some Lasagna and Shut Up!

On narcissism, the art of conversation, and making time for others

I HAVE A VERY DEAR FRIEND whom I've known for years. We now live several hundred miles apart and don't see each other all that often, but we make it a habit to talk on the phone at regular intervals.

A few weeks ago it occurred to me that we hadn't talked in quite a long time, so I called her at home. Of course, I got an answering machine. "Hello, please leave me your name and number and the reason for your call, and I'll get back to you as soon as I can."

Two days later she called me from her car phone. "Hi, it's me. I'm so sorry I haven't called in such a long time. Things here were just insane! I've been working so hard it's unbelievable. I worked all weekend on a project, and when I wasn't working, I had to take the kids to a birthday party and two playdates. I haven't had a minute to call. I'm so overwhelmed I just don't know what to do."

I didn't know what to say to her. This is truly absurd. My friend hasn't called me for a month, then she takes the first ten minutes of a conversation to tell me that she's too busy to talk to me. What kind of crap is that?

But you know what? It's not crap. Yes, it always feels like you're being fed a line when someone says they couldn't find five minutes to call you. But the truth is that these days we really are all feeling overwhelmed. Remember the statistics: we work more hours, and have less leisure time, than any society on this planet. Our lives have become so hectic and overscheduled and insanely paced that stopping to make a phone call—even to someone you really love and want to talk to—often feels like just too big an additional task to take on in the course of a day.

I don't know when this started, and I don't know that there are any hard-and-firm statistics to bear me out on this, but I swear that there has been a massive increase in the last several years in the amount that people talk about how busy they are. It's an epidemic! You can't make a phone call or see a friend or even talk to relatives without hearing people whine on and on

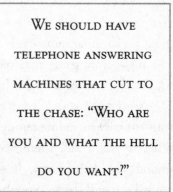

We should have telephone answering machines that cut to the chase: "Who are you and what the hell do you want?"

about how tired they are and how they have no time to do anything.

And, it seems to me, they talk about it so much because it's true. Everybody is working harder, and when they're not working, everybody is scheduling any scrap of free time they may have for the next six months.

So when they're not whining about how tired they are, they're whining about how they have no time to see you. And it feels as if they're proud to tell you so. "Oh, I'm dying to get together with you, but I have a business trip coming up, and then it's little Josie's recital; then we're going up to Vermont for the weekend; and, God, then it's end-of-the-year budgets—that'll take several weeks of working weekends."

I feel like saying, "How about after I'm dead? Would that be good for you?"

When my women friends and I want to get together for lunch, we have to call in Price Waterhouse to figure out a time we can all do it. You should see the juggling of dates that goes on! I think the United Nations Security Council could get together more easily.

It's a crazy thing that our society has done to itself. And it seems to me a major shift in our societal structure.

Years ago, we all lived in communities that were close-knit—usually including family members that lived nearby. When I was a kid, there was always a group of people around who helped out. If someone was in trouble, or needed a hand, there were always several people to go to. Neighbors would drop in and sit for coffee, and mothers often shopped together or cooked meals together. Today, no one drops in; if we see someone walking up our driveway, we have a nervous breakdown!

> WE GO TO HALLMARK AND WE BUY PICTURE FRAMES THAT SAY WORDS LIKE "FAMILY" AND "FRIENDSHIP" ON THEM. THEN WE PUT PHOTOS IN THEM OF PEOPLE WE'RE TOO BUSY TO SEE.

And the extended family was always there, making everyone feel part of something when they came home. It wasn't always easy, you didn't always want your relatives talking about the outfit you wore to work today, or whether or not they liked what your new boyfriend did for a living. But at least people were there. Someone noticed. Human beings were watching and interacting with you. If you felt bad, someone was there for you to talk to about it. If you got too full of yourself, someone was there to bring you back down to earth. If it was just an ordinary day, maybe your grandmother would have a plate of cookies to make you feel just a little bit nurtured.

Intimate human communication was an important part of life. Then someone got it into his head that communication had to be made more efficient.

Over the last fifteen years or so, you haven't been able to turn around without hearing about the development of a new gadget to help you communicate with other people. We're all obsessed with communication: we have to get messages to one another at all hours of the day and night, anywhere in the world, in written or spoken form, with or without photographic or musical accompaniment.

Think about it. It started with answering machines. You'd call someone at home and if they were out you'd get what was basically a tape recorder instead. "Hi, this is Loretta and I'm not home right now. Leave me a message and I'll call you back."

I resisted getting one of those machines for years because, frankly, I didn't see the big deal. If I wasn't home, so what? Whoever wanted me would call back.

But of course, within a couple of years *everybody* had one, and you were made to feel like a pariah if you didn't. In fact, people made it sound as if I was being wildly inconsiderate for refusing to get one. After all, my refusal was making other people call me more than once. I was wasting their time! I was making them call repeatedly because I was too selfish to get an answering machine.

So, like everyone else, I got an answering machine.

Then, answering machines grew up and became voice mail. For people at home, that didn't make a huge difference, except for the fact that you no longer even had to come home to listen to your messages. If you were out at the supermarket and wanted to know if somebody called you, you could stop at a telephone and call your voice mail system to see. You had to first dial a number for access, then enter your ten-digit number, then a password. The whole thing took five minutes. Of course, I would find myself stopping whatever else I was doing every ten minutes or so to call in and check my voice mail and see if anybody called.

This, again, was meant to save time.

Big companies, of course, were among the first to really use voice mail systems. And, God, what efficient time-savers they have turned out to be. Last week I had to call the phone company to complain that my voice mail wasn't working, and it took me twenty-seven minutes to finally get to talk to someone who could help me.

First the voice mail system welcomed me, in a deep melodious voice that sounded suspiciously like Darth Vader, and told me that I was very important to them.

It then asked me to identify myself with a twenty-two digit identification code that could be found in the upper left-hand corner of my bill.

Then, after I entered the number, it asked me to choose from one of seven possible reasons that I was calling. The fact that my voice mail wasn't working was not one of the options so I didn't know what to press. While I was hesitating, it repeated the op-

WHEN MY GRANDMOTHER HAD TO CALL THE PHONE COMPANY, SOMEONE WOULD ANSWER THE PHONE. SHE'D SAY, "THIS IS FRANCESCA ARICO. HERE'S MY PHONE NUMBER," AND WHOEVER ANSWERED THE PHONE WOULD BE ABLE TO HELP HER.

tions, but I swear it sounded a little angrier this time. I was still a little confused about which one to press, but when I paused this time, the damned thing hung up on me.

So I had to call back.

It again told me how important I am.

I went through it all again, including entering the twenty-two digit number, and this time I chose "customer service" from the seven options.

I was told that all the representatives were busy serving other customers (all of whom, presumably, were also important) and that my call would be answered shortly. In fact, it went on to say, my call would be answered in approximately twelve minutes.

So I pulled out the book I was reading, and sat and read while the twelve minutes passed. Phone rage is just not my style.

After fourteen minutes (not that I was counting), a customer service representative answered and asked me for my twenty-two digit identification number. I did stop and wonder why the hell I had to enter it into the phone pad if I had to read it to the live person again anyway, but I didn't press the issue. I read it to her again. I explained my problem. She told me that I didn't need customer service at all, I needed technical support and that I should please hold on, she would connect me.

I was connected with the voice mail for technical support. I was asked to enter my twenty-two digit identification number. I was then told that all technical service representatives were busy serving other important customers, but that my call would be answered in approximately fourteen minutes.

My voice mail still isn't working.

But, who needs voice mail anyway, because today . . . Ah, today! Even voice mail is an antiquated thing of the past because now, you need never be unreachable. No one need ever leave you a message because now you have a cell phone. Wherever you are, walking on the street, shopping at the supermarket, playing bridge with friends, at a funeral mass, making love to your partner at a quiet getaway spot, right in the middle of the "to be or not to be" speech in a live production of Shakespeare's *Hamlet*: RRRing!

Instant relentless communication, whenever and wherever you choose. Now you really can save time, by being interrupted in the middle of whatever else you might have been doing. You can have conversations in your car while you might otherwise be concentrating on the traffic conditions. You can have conversations on one of those little microphone attachments while you're walking down the street, and have people look at you strangely and cross to the other side. You can have conversations on commuter trains and buses, where the people sitting alongside of you truly appreciate the opportunity to listen in on your personal conversations.

But, of course, I'm being a little silly here. Most people don't want to be interrupted in the middle of important life events. They know that there are certain times that it's just inappropriate to have a cellular phone conversation, so they turn their phones off. And if someone tries to reach them then? The calls go to cellular voice mail.

Can anyone in their right mind actually believe that the advances in communication have saved us time? I think they've cost us hours every week just in checking messages. Many people have to check their home voice mail, their work voice mail, and their cellular voice mail. If they're expecting an important call, they probably check often. How much time has that wasted from the days when, if you missed a call, well, they'd just have to try you back (and, of course, it costs a lot of money, too, because remember, every time you call for your voice mail messages, you've made another phone call. The phone company ain't stupid . . .)?

So we keep coming up with new ways to communicate with one another. We carry pagers that vibrate. You're walking down the street and all of a sudden you get a thrill in the nether regions. In the old days that might have made you think of a different kind of communication but today, no, it's just your pager going off.

And what happens when you get paged? You stop whatever you're doing and call someone back. You desperately hope that you don't get the voice mail.

When all else fails, and you've left voice mail messages, and you've paged, and you've tried the cell phone number, there's only one last resort:

You send an e-mail. The e-mail says, "please call me."

And what if, finally, you actually do get connected and on the other side of the phone wire is the real living, breathing person you've been waiting so long to talk to? Two minutes into the call you're interrupted by "call waiting."

Isn't this nuts? Instead of living in communities in which we actually talk to one another, we live in one big community in which we leave high-tech messages for one another and seem to never actually communicate.

We used to come home and have family and extended family waiting to ask us how our day was, now we all come home and nobody's there. There's no one to say, "I'm so glad to see you," or "Gee, you did great today." Instead, we listen to our answering machines. In order to have real connection with our larger extended families, we have to place phone calls and play tag for three days in order to get an answer.

Maybe we send an e-mail instead, and think of that as a warm intimate human interaction.

And I think that's the reason we all schedule ourselves to death, and we walk around with our palm pilots filled with 575 phone numbers and e-mail addresses and our daily appointment calendar for the next five years. We do it in order to fill the void. Instead of a life filled with human beings and conversation, we fill it up with a to-do list and virtual communication.

You used to feel important because your grandmother told you she loved you, and that you were terrific. These days, you feel important because every minute of every day is taken up with things you have to do! Since you're booked solid, you must be important!

It's such a sad way to live, but most of us fall into the trap. We think that filling up every minute of our day is life-affirming, but way too often those things really are life-draining. Instead of giving ourselves room to have real close human connection, we fill our time with business pursuits and social obligations. We fill our days with so much, in fact, that we're always exhausted.

My own husband lives this way! He has bought me organizers, palm pilots, filofaxes and day timers. He is obsessed, like so many people are, with schedules. He's not happy unless every moment of the day is packaged, sliced, written down, premeditated, planned, measured and calculated for.

I'm not well organized, I know it. I thrive in chaos. I have piles of papers here and there, I do this and that, I put numbers on things, I always have a vague memory of where I put something, I hem and haw. And you know what? I get a lot

> I WANT SOMEONE TO INVENT A FUN TIMER. *What's a fun timer?* WE HAVE A DAY TIMER, RIGHT? THIS IS A THING THAT TELLS YOU WHEN IT'S TIME TO HAVE FUN. BECAUSE THESE DAYS, NO ONE BELIEVES THAT THEY HAVE THE RIGHT TO HAVE FUN UNTIL THEY FINISH EVERYTHING THAT'S IN THEIR ORGANIZER.

done. And those organizers my husband tries to get me to use? I can't even find them!

I don't care. I don't want to write everything down. I don't want to be organized. Because then I feel that I have no creative outlet, no spontaneity. I feel trapped. I feel tied to that list.

But for my husband? God, if he doesn't have that list, I think he feels, I don't know . . . *confused*. I say to him, "why don't you try to do number ten first? Instead of number one." But no, he can't do number ten till this afternoon. I take my walk in the afternoon. Why? Why can't you take a walk this morning? Because I'm getting my hair cut this morning. What would happen if you exchanged the two? Would you blow up?

My grandmother didn't have an organizer.

What did she do? When she needed something, she went to the store. She said, "I'm leaving." And then, when she returned, she said, "I'm back!" If someone was there they heard her. If no one was around, nobody knew. And she was content with that. She did what she had to do, and she accomplished everything she wanted to, without writing it down in her palm pilot and downloading it onto the Internet.

Our obsession with schedules makes us crazy, don't you think?

And if we have kids, we do it to them, too. Do you know families that have young children today? Those kids need their *own* palm pilots! They go to school five days a week, then on the other days they take after-school music classes, or gymnastic classes, or ballet classes or chess or art or whatever. Sometimes three afternoons a week they have after-school activities scheduled.

So when do they get to go out and play with their friends? Well, they don't! They make playdates for two weeks from Thursday.

And their parents take them to all these places, so that gives the parents even more rushing around to do.

All-in-all, it gives them yet another thing to complain about. Even more! "Oh, I'm so tired!"

Of course, the thing that many of us don't recognize is that talking about the problem in and of itself makes the problem worse.

This is true for two reasons: first, it's inherent in the human brain that the more you talk about something, the more you'll feel it. Do you doubt that? Say to yourself that you're sad fifteen times in a row. How does that make you feel?

So the more that we complain about being tired, and being busy, and being overwhelmed, the more our brain will feel tired, and overwhelmed. It's like we're living through the exhaustion, and then living it again. We force our bodies to keep feeling the pain over and over and over, so they can never recover.

But second, and I think even more disturbing, is this: **Who the hell cares how tired you are?** Can you think of a subject that is more boring for someone else to have to listen to?

How do you respond when someone goes on and on

about how exhausted and overwhelmed they are? It seems to me you have two choices: you can say, "I feel so sorry for you." Or you can say "I know, I feel tired and exhausted too." How dull is that? You can just put one another to sleep while you're talking.

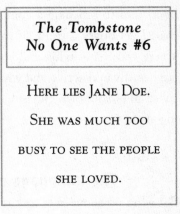

The Tombstone No One Wants #6

HERE LIES JANE DOE.

SHE WAS MUCH TOO

BUSY TO SEE THE PEOPLE

SHE LOVED.

When someone calls me and then goes on and on about how tired he is, and how much he has to do, and how many other things he needs to do before he can see me—how do you think I feel? I feel lousy and taken for granted; all I can think of is "so why did you call me?" This has absolutely nothing to do with me or with anything that I can share with you. Go look in the mirror; that's the only person who can share this stuff with you.

On top of that, I've got to tell the truth here: when I listen to someone going on about how hard they work and how tired they are, it's hard to feel sorry for them. I don't know about you, maybe you can have more empathy than I do in this situation, but I feel harangued! And then I feel like the last thing I want to do is give any compassion or empathy to someone who has consciously chosen to work themselves too hard. I have a lot of compassion for people who are ill, for people who face real obstacles in their lives, or for people who are doing challenging things with gusto. But when someone consciously decides to work endless hours and to schedule a complicated social life on top of that, I get angry. I think, if this is the life you want, fine. You're earning a living and you're traveling and your kids are healthy and active and you're involved in a swirl of activity all of your own choosing. Just shut up and stop whining about it.

The Language of Narcissism

But whining about overwork is only a small piece of what I think is a bigger problem. I'm worried that our isolated and narcissistic way of life, and our continued reliance on virtual forms of communication, is diminishing our ability to hold real conversations. The art of it seems to be fading. Instead of enriching conversations, people seem to have an incessant need to disclose those things which are irritating, overwhelming, fatiguing and nauseating.

I've spoken above about the most pervasive form of narcissistic communication: whining. But that's just one of many variants. The other one that drives me crazy and that is also an epidemic these days is the way people talk on and on about the chemical composition of the food they put in their mouths, and its effect on their health.

Again: who the hell cares?

Doesn't it seem like no one can eat a hamburger these days without saying, "oh, well, I guess I'm going to have to work out for a week now." Or "there goes my cholesterol level."

Listen, I'm all for people wanting to take care of their

bodies, but do I have to listen to it twenty-four hours a day? It's got nothing to do with me. It's narcissistic. It's all about how someone feels about what they're putting in their own mouths and, excuse me, but what exactly does that have to do with me? Nothing!

If you want to eat something, eat it. If you don't want to eat it, don't eat it. But we don't all have to listen to a recitation of the effect it's going to have on your HDL Cholesterol level.

Just have some lasagna and shut up!

People talk on and on about how difficult their commute is. "I was stuck in traffic for a half an hour." What should I say to that? Thank goodness it wasn't for a whole hour? What's the point?

See, I think the issue is that our society has gone so far away from a communal "we" mindset to a narcissistic "I" mindset, that the topics of conversation have very often become small and limited. We talk about the clothes we're wearing, the hair products we use, the things we own, the vacations we're taking, and all the annoying things that are getting in our way.

We don't think about what might engage the people we're talking to. We don't think of the community, we think of ourselves.

Here's another example of this: Have you noticed that everyone these days knows everything? I can't have a conversation with another person without hearing "Oh, I know that." "Yes, I heard that." "I know that already." "I just read about that." "I just saw something about that."

Everybody's an expert on everything. And more importantly, they want you to know it.

Everybody's read the newest magazines, the latest books, they've seen today's website, they watch CNN, or they listen to the radio, and they read three newspapers.

You can't tell anybody anything and have them say "Geez! That's interesting!" It doesn't matter how fascinating the story or how fresh the information, before you're finished talking, it'll be *"Yeah, I heard that."*

We're overloaded with so much information that everybody has to always feel that they're on top of what's happening. Everything these days is a sound bite, and transmission of information is instant. So wherever you look you get the same twenty bits of information streaming at you. *"A new study says that if mice eat their weight in sundried tomatoes, they get colon cancer."* Before you know it, it's there on the front page of your web portal, it's on the ticker that goes by on the highway billboard as you drive home, it's on the all-news radio station you listen to, it's on the all-news TV station you watch, it's in the afternoon papers and by the time it's three hours old, everybody in the world is talking about it in nineteen languages. They're already bored with the news in Hong Kong before you get home.

So you walk in the door and your wife asks you "Did you hear about the mice . . ."

"Yeah, sundried tomatoes. Colon cancer. *I heard that.*"

Along the same lines, it seems to me that what little dialogue we do have with others is often polluted with little dismissive buzzwords that, to my mind, stop conversation dead.

"Oh, puh-leeze."

"Don't go there."

"Same old, same old."

"Whatever!"

"Yadda, yadda, yadda."

"Been there, done that."

I feel like saying, "OK, so just drop dead; then you won't have to do anything. You'll have been there, you'll have done that, and that's that."

Using buzzword phrases like this in place of real dialogue and conversation eclipses having real contact with someone. **You could just grunt**.

Those particular phrases, while perhaps on the surface meant as a way to elicit a smile because of their familiarity, are so filled with ennui, so reek with boredom, that they feel diminutive and keep people separate from any real human interaction and warmth. They emanate with the sentiment "I have better things to do. This bores me."

In every way, it feels more and more like we're all walking around in our own little plastic bubble and never really touching one another. We say things that keep people away instead of drawing them in. Instead of holding conversations, we perform soliloquies.

Even in the big mainstream movies, there is no dialogue anymore (they're too busy giving us lessons on how to blow things up, run cars off bridges or shoot 300 people in an hour and a half). Everything is short, snappy lines that sound like they've been written and rewritten and edited twelve times by professional comedians. They don't talk like real people used to talk. So, we get the signal everywhere: conversation is boring.

When, of course, the truth is that conversation is the glue of life. And it can be the most fascinating, intense, enriching and exciting way to spend a few hours you could ever experience. But it takes time.

Conversation is about listening, responding, and engaging with another person. It's about opening up lines of communication, not shutting them down. And we do that by talking about subjects that will be interesting to the other person, and make them want to talk to you.

Narcissistic subjects shut down conversation.

IF YOU FIND YOURSELF RELYING ON THESE SUBJECTS IN CONVERSATION, YOU SHOULD PROBABLY JUST SHUT UP!

- ❖ things you eat

- ❖ things you don't eat

- ❖ what you drink

- ❖ what you won't drink

- ❖ how tired you are

- ❖ when you go to sleep

- ❖ how much exercise you get

- ❖ how much fiber you eat

- ❖ how hard you work

- ❖ how much weight you lost (or gained)

- ❖ what your cholesterol count is

- ❖ how long you can last on the StairMaster

- ❖ what vitamin supplements you take

It's amazing to me how often these subjects really are the source of conversation, if not the full extent of entire conversations. They're so mundane and so boring. Yet, time and time again I sit with people and these are the things we end up talking about. It makes me nuts.

Engaging conversations are about things that go beyond just the basic food-and-shelter subjects mentioned above. Listen, it's not so interesting and surprising that you ate today. Everybody ate something today. Unless you did something wildly extraordinary, nobody cares about your intake.

But, if what you ate was the most magnificent chocolate soufflé, prepared in a way that was truly unusual and extraordinary—and you happen to be talking to someone whom you know would appreciate such a magnificent culinary creation—then, yes, describe every mouthwatering bite with flair and gusto. Because you're using it to bring the other person in, you're sharing with them something that you think they might like.

And instead of talking about what a hard time you had getting home from work that day, being stuck in traffic for an hour, talk about what an interesting book on tape you listened to, or the beautiful piece of music you heard that the other person might like, or the discussion on the radio talk show that you found fascinating.

It's about finding the nugget of something interesting, or significant, or joyful that you can share with someone else. What you want to do is find the thing that will enrich someone else's life, and when you do that, it will enrich your life as well.

What happens is that good conversation raises the bar; it brings richness both ways. You learn about what brings joy and happiness and growth into other people's lives, and they learn the same about you. And you're both enriched.

You have to go toward your passions when you're around other people; that's the way to create intimacy. The things to share in conversation are the things that really energize you, the things you can't live without, the exciting details that make you feel alive and tingling.

When we're trying to communicate with other people, we have to leave the mundane behind. We have to reach toward the things that constitute the better life, the richer life, the life we want rather than the life we sometimes feel stuck in. We all have things in our lives that annoy us and enrage us, but what's the point in talking more about them? So that they can enrage and annoy us all over again? And annoy and enrage the people around us, too?

Good conversation should be about things that feel special to you, that are beautiful, that are enriching. Think about what is important in your life: what are the things you can't live without? For me, those things are fresh air, fascinating people, movement, laughter.

For others, those things may include art, theater, music, politics, sports, literature, nature. Those are the things you need to share with people around you. Let them see the best that you can be, the most interesting and passionate person that exists inside of you.

It takes a little daring, because trying to stay present and talk about the things that truly engage us gets closer to the soul, and it's often scary for people to expose that much of themselves. It's so much easier to talk in clichés about our annoying boss or our workout routine or how much water we drank today. But that's the easy way out, and the easy way out never pays off.

If you want to really connect with other people, dig deep and talk about the things that really engross you, and you'll find that it will also captivate them. Think of the way children communicate, before they have learned the rules of adulthood. Kids hold back nothing, and while you probably don't want to share your excitement over your last bowel movement the way a three-year-old might, you can and should share the wonder you feel looking at a beautiful sunset, or the fun you had playing a game with other people, or how amazed you felt at watching the way a spider walks, or an eagle flies, or a bridge hangs there so gracefully.

Use conversation as a way to share the beauty you see in the world, not the petty annoyances of life. In its best form, conversation is an art that enriches all parties.

Try to think of ways that all the gadgets for communication could actually be used to enhance the art instead of detracting from it, the way they often do. You can send someone an e-mail saying: "I just read the most amazing article and I'm attaching a copy. Let's talk about it tonight at ten after the kids are asleep."

How about calling someone's voice mail and just telling a funny personal story (forwarding e-mail jokes do not count! That's impersonal)?

Can you show someone how much you care about them by saying: "I don't care what's on my schedule. You tell me when you'd like to see me, and I'll be there."?

Can you also let them know how much you need them by saying: "I really need to see you soon. Please."

That's communication.

Take a Socrates Break.
Don't ask me; ask yourself:

❖ *Do you find yourself calling people at off-hours because you'd rather leave a message than actually talk to the person you're calling?*

❖ *Do you look at everything written in your organizer and shake your head in dismay? Have you ever thought of just erasing the damned thing?*

❖ *Do you find yourself feeling uncomfortable when you're in a deep conversation, trying to find ways to get out of it?*

❖ *How many voice mails do you really need?*

❖ *When trying to plan an event with a friend, do you tell them all the things you have to do first, or do you try to make it sound as if seeing them is your priority?*

❖ *How often do you talk to people about how much weight you've lost, or gained?*

❖ *Do you feel afraid when someone knocks on your door, "Who the hell is that?"*

❖ *If you carry a pager or a cell phone: how important is it, really, that you never miss a call? Are you a trauma surgeon? Is anyone going to die if you wait to get home to get the message?*

❖ *Do you feel that you have to fill up every moment of your child's time with after school activities?*

❖ *Are you more comfortable telling friends about everything that is wrong with your life rather than what is good about your life? Why do you suppose that is?*

7

Women Are from Venus, Men Are from Hunger

On the differences between the sexes

CAN I ASK YOU A FAVOR? If you ever run into my husband, don't tell him about this chapter. You know how men are: they don't like it when you talk about them. But I want to make a confession, here, and I can't do it without talking about my marriage. That means talking about my husband. So, please, keep it to yourself.

My husband and I are in our early sixties, and we straddle two generations who believe very different things. Today's generation believes, and rightly so, that men and women are completely equal in all things: that no expectations should be levied against people of either sex. And, certainly, that no opportunities should be denied to anyone because of their sex.

My grandparents' generation, however, thought that

was an absolutely ridiculous notion. To people of that generation, there was men's work and there was women's work, and if anybody chose to do the work of the other sex, well, something about them was not quite right.

Our grandparents' generation still lived as if they were in the caves. Right? I never saw my grandfather change a diaper. He didn't get up in the middle of the night when one of the kids needed to be fed or had a bad dream. That was the women's work. He went off to the office every day, came home at six, sat down with the family for dinner, then sat in the living room and read the paper or listened to the radio.

When my grandmother wanted to have conversations about other people in the neighborhood, or about the relatives, just to tell stories and have an entertaining chat, the last person she would turn to was my grandfather. She knew he wouldn't be interested; it wasn't something that women in those days did with men. They did it with other women. My grandmother had a group of old ladies in the neighborhood who I used to think of as the three witches from *Macbeth*—only they'd do their "double double toil and trouble" around the macaroni pot. They would sit in the kitchen, day-in and day-out, telling stories about the families in the neighborhood.

It was right out of *The Flintstones!*

Now, here I am, just a generation later, and I've got a career and I'm out on the road, and I'm writing books. I don't sit home and gossip with my cronies.

I work. I work hard, I travel a lot, and I'm not often

home to make my husband dinner or to greet him in a little pink apron with a martini and his slippers in my hand. I'm often not home at all.

And while he is a modern man, and is delighted that I have a career of my own, and is proud of my accomplishments, I know that deep down he wishes I were there to hand him the newspaper and cook breakfast. Why wouldn't he? That's the way he saw his mother treat his father, and the way he was treated when he was a boy. It's what he was brought up to expect.

Yes, he's happy to see me work. But what he really wants is June Cleaver who happens to run Microsoft on the side.

And for me: I'm a little embarrassed to admit this, but I'm completely a victim of the flip side of this. I saw my mother and my grandmother stay at home and raise the family and do the things that felt more instinctively right for them. I go out and work and bring home money—and I'm happy to do it. But deep down I'm feeling: *why should I have to share my money with you?* I want to be taken care of: I want my hunter to bring home all the money that the household needs and I want to be able to do whatever I want with mine.

Usually, when we have stresses in our marriage, this is the subject matter. And I know, from the people I talk to on the road and from the response I get from audiences when I talk about this subject that my husband and I are far from alone on this.

There's a terrific book that I picked up about a year ago

while traveling in Ireland, a book first published in Australia, but now available in the U.S., called *Why Men Don't Listen and Women Can't Read Maps.*

The authors of this book, Barbara and Allen Pease, have done a great deal of research into the biological reasons and psychological patterning that, over the centuries, have contributed to making men and women different from one another. And it all started with the cavemen. For me, they make a lot of sense about what's going on inside our heads.

Think about what it was like for the cavemen, long before anyone ever read *Cosmo.* Men were the hunters. They would go out together in packs, searching for meat to feed the tribe. Women were the nurturers and the gatherers. They stayed home, raised the children, prepared meals, kept the cave in order, searched for the fruits and nuts, and worked as a community with the other women.

It was simple and clear. Everyone knew what was expected of them.

During the tens of thousands of years that it took for men to grow into their biological role as hunters, they learned an important lesson: when you're hunting for food, you have to be stealthlike, focused. Your life is on the line when you're on the hunt, as is the survival of your tribe. You don't take your mind off the prize for a second, because if you do, the animal could get away. Or, if the animal in question is bigger than you, it could eat *you* instead of the other way around.

And, without question, one thing that you did not do

while you were on the scent in the jungle, looking for your prey, is talk.

If you blab, they'll hear you. If they hear you, they'll either run, or they'll find you and kill you. Either way, no dinner.

So men went out together in silence—whether they were in a pack or alone—and remained silent and furtive and focused until they completed the task at hand. They stalked their prey individually (because a big group loses the power of surprise) and each one hoped that he'd be the one to bag the kill. He could then be the one to pound on his chest and show off: *I won the prize.*

The only thing men like better than to be quiet is to show off. The caveman who had the biggest, uh, club—the one who brought home the most meat—was the one who was most adored. And it's no surprise he was so adored: thanks to him, everybody ate.

So, when the men returned from the hunt, they would sit around the fire after having consumed a good meal and they would reflect on their day of pursuit. They do not, however, rehash every step they took or every track they mistakenly followed before they got on the right trail. No, their basic nature is to remain quiet and focused. Now the task is to feel relaxed and peaceful. Why ruin it by having to talk? Their male reflection takes the form of a grunt of pleasure. Maybe, someone passes gas. The one who killed the mammoth sits there with his arms behind his neck, basking in the glory and admiration bestowed upon him.

This is well-documented male behavior. You can see

the same thing taking place today anywhere in the country on Super Bowl Sunday.

But the cavewomen! Their nature is completely different. They're social beings, they stay home and take care of the children, the meals, and the family. They live in the "village" with one another and communicate readily—because that is the way that they know how to get things done. They negotiate and collaborate with one another on preparing the meals and gathering the grains. It takes the entire group of women to make the community work.

Can you imagine what would go on if the women were sent out to hunt? While the men stayed silently focused for hours on their task, the women couldn't stand it for two seconds. Can't you just hear the conversations?

"So, are you enjoying the hunt?"

"What do you think, will we get something today? The weather isn't so great for hunting."

"Have you done this before? This is my third hunt."

"How do you like my hunting dress? I love yours, where did you get it?"

"Girls, I vote that we stop for a minute and have a snack and pee."

And then, would they ever really manage to kill what they set out to hunt? Can't you picture a group of women out there in the jungle, cooing "isn't that behemoth cute? Look, there's its mother. Let's just take some roots back and make a stew."

And if the men were left behind to gather and nurture? They'd sit and pound away at the grain for days, trying to figure out how to turn it into flour. But would they stop and ask somebody how to do it? Never!

The patterns of male and female behavior are by nature very different. Men, whatever it is that they happen to be doing, treat it as if they are setting out on the hunt. They go after their prey, and they are intent on bagging it. They are focused on completing their task. The only thing that is important to them at that moment is the activity. They are not interested in sidebars; they don't want to know how anyone is feeling about what they're doing, or what anyone is wearing, or what happened on the last hunt two weeks ago.

They want to bring home the fresh hunk of meat.

Women, on the other hand, are multi-taskers. When they were in the caves, they had a child in one hand, and at the same time they were cooking the meals, talking to the other women in the caves and yelling at the other kids to stop playing near the fire. Meanwhile, they were weaving together a tapestry of stories and expressing feelings. They were the history makers; they created and passed down the traditions.

So, now it's today. And you're sitting and watching your husband with the TV remote control in his hands, and he's totally absorbed in what he's watching on the tube. *Totally absorbed.* **He's hunting**. You have to beat him over the head to get his attention, because you want to tell him that you're going to the mall. He doesn't give a crap about that. What's that got to do with him? He can only focus on one thing at a time, and right now, it's watching television. In his biological core he knows that if he's not fully focused, if he turns his back on that hemorrhoid commercial for just a fraction of a second, that wooly mammoth could trample him. We women want him to care about what we're saying and what we need from him. But it's not in his nature to care when he's doing something else. He can only focus on one task at a time.

So, what happens? You go off with some friends to the mall and when you come home you want to tell him everything that happened. You drove there with Gloria, and she got a new car as a birthday present, who knew that her husband was doing so well? And while you were there you ran into Sally who was there with her daughter Ruby who just got into Harvard but, it's too bad, she's put on a lot of weight and they couldn't find anything they liked in her size.

He's thinking, "What the hell do you want? What's the point?"

Men are more interested in getting to the point. Women are interested in the peripheral stuff that gives flavor, richness and texture to life.

As a general rule, that seems to just be the way it is.

The brains of men and women are patterned differently, and it happened over tens of thousands of years when we lived in tribes in the wilderness. Just like we've passed down genes from generation to generation that, for example, have made us taller over the centuries, so have we passed down genes that seem to pattern us for certain types of behavior. For hundreds of thousands of years, men and women believed that certain duties were prescribed for each of them. It worked. Buried down somewhere in our little heads is the belief (however mistaken) that it's still supposed to work.

Now, though, we rightly believe that this kind of patterned behavior is no longer appropriate or proper. We like to believe that it's an ideal world, and that men and women should be equal in every way. We think that men should share the housework duties, be fully engaged parents, and be sensitive and articulate about feelings. We also think that women should share the responsibility for earning a living and protecting the tribe. In other words, we should all be able to be the hunters and the gatherers and the nurturers.

It's a good concept, and we're on our way to making it a reality. But let's face it: we've got a long way to go to work out the kinks. If you figure that it took a hundred thousand years or so for our brains to develop in such a way that men naturally understand that they are the hunters and women naturally understand that they are the nurturers, it's unlikely we'll be able to overcome that patterning before at least a few more seasons of *Dharma and Greg*.

Think about these very obvious ways that men and women are different. They are so clear that they've become clichés and an endless source of material for comedians—but think them through for a moment. Why are they such stereotypes? It's because they are true. Why are they so true? Because we're patterned that way . . .

Men Don't Ask for Directions

Of course not. If a man stops to ask for directions, the animal he's stalking will kill him. Not to mention that it is a clear indication that he is out of control and needs help. It literally forces him to make the admission, perhaps to another male, that "I'm lost." What could be farther from the male's natural desire to best all others and come out the winner? Women, on the other hand, have no qualms about asking others for help. In fact, they can't get enough of it! Women know that asking other people for help not only gets them what they need, it makes for human connection and communication which nurtures all concerned.

Women Go to the Bathroom in Groups

And why not? It's a bonding ritual—it's like staying home in the cave and working together to make the night's meal. Women like to do things together and have other women around; everything is a collaborative effort. Even peeing. It doesn't matter if a woman really needs to empty her bladder or not, she'll go to keep her friend company. Why not? Men, on the other hand, want to perform whatever their task happens to be in silence and get it over with. Why in the world would they want another man to come with them to the john? Exactly how will that help them to complete the appointed task—to empty their bladder? To a man, it's the most absurd idea in the world.

Men Don't Notice the Details

Not long ago I bought a new oriental rug for the dining room. The rug we had in there had gotten kind of frayed and old, so I bought one that was much bigger and a different color.

My husband walked over it for six months before he noticed something had changed. And from what I see, he's not all that unusual. A man can go for days and not notice that his wife has changed her hairdo, or that there's a new chair in the living room.

It makes sense: that's the stuff on the periphery. But put something in the room that is related to one of his primary drives and he'll notice it in an instant. If he's sitting in a meeting at work and his boss leans over to whisper in the ear of one of his competitors, he'll notice that. If a woman fifty feet away is not wearing a bra, he'll notice that.

Women, on the other hand, notice everything. She'll notice if the guy has parted his hair a half inch to the left, she'll notice if her girlfriend is wearing a new shade of toenail polish, she'll notice if someone in the office is looking a little depressed that day.

Well, of course she will. Women are programmed for detail: they compile the information and tell the stories. They are interested in the periphery. Men are interested only in the task that they have to complete.

And while we're speaking of that . . .

Sex

What do men do after sex? For the most part, if they're married, they fall asleep. If they're single, they usually can't wait to get their pants on and get the hell out of there.

They have completed their task. Their seed is planted, thank you very much, now what's next?

Women want to snuggle up; they want to chat, "was that good for you?" They use sex, like they use virtually everything else, as a way to enhance closeness and communication. They feel more bonded to men after sex than before, they feel warm and loving. They want that encounter to have been meaningful to both of them. They want intimacy and they want to feel nurtured. To them, those moments after sex are an idyllic romantic experience. They stare at the ceiling and feel enrapt by the spiritual, intimate emotions.

The man stares at the ceiling and thinks "I wonder how that fly can walk upside down that way?"

Men and Women Laugh at Different Things

It's true. Think about it:

Get a group of guys together at a ball game after a few beers. What do you hear? "Who'd you bet on? The loser?" "Remember when you had abs under that gut?" "Maybe when you get a real job you can sit up here with the big boys." They rag on one another. They all see humor in playful one-upmanship that points out the other guy's flaws.

Yes, it's usually good-natured—and no one goes off and

> IT TOOK NATURE TENS OF THOUSANDS OF YEARS OF EVOLUTION TO WORK OUT THAT IN THE HUMAN SPECIES, MEN DO THE HUNTING AND WOMEN DO THE NURTURING. DO WE REALLY THINK WE CAN OVERCOME THOSE FEELINGS IN ONE GENERATION?

cries in his beer. The humor is very clearly based on their common understanding that it is critically important to men to make themselves look good, often at the expense of one another. Putting the other guy down and excluding him from the inner circle is seen as funny. *You couldn't catch a woolly mammoth if your life depended on it.* Subtext: *but of course I can.*

Can you imagine for one moment a group of women making fun of one another in the same way? *What are you wearing that black dress for, to cover your fat ass?* Of course not. Nine times out of ten, what you'll much more likely hear is a woman making fun of herself: *of course I'm wearing a black dress, have you seen the size of my ass?*

Closely tied into this topic is the fact that:

Men Talk Themselves Up;
Women Talk Themselves Down

Get a group of guys together to talk about last week's golf game. What will you hear? Unless it's talk about the weather, more often than not you'll hear guys brag about how well they did: "best game I ever played." "You should have seen me hit right to the green on that seventeenth hole. It was beautiful."

Men like to reinforce their dominant position. Whenever they're in a position of having won, of beating out a competitor or of leading the tribe to victory, they want everyone to know it and to admire them.

Women, on the other hand, usually feel very uncomfortable in similar situations and do the opposite. If they're talking to other women about their golf game, they're much more likely to say things like "Oh, I just couldn't hit for anything that day." Or "I should never wear those golfing pants, they make my legs look fat." Why? Because women know that talking about their own insecurities will draw other women in and make them feel instinctively comfortable. Women want to bond with other women, they want to complete the circle and create an aura of mutual nurturance. They look for equanimity: how can we all feel good about one another and achieve equality?

Men also crave bonding with other men, but their natural way of trying to create closeness is by the winning of the other's respect and the clarification of where they stand in the pecking order. That's why men can play three sets of racquetball and never say a word to each other but end the day feeling like they've become best friends. They have each showed the other what they're made of, and assuming neither one embarrassed himself, they've earned each other's respect as competitors. They've never once had to discuss feeling "bloated."

So, you may be asking (especially if you're a man):

What's the Point?

The point is this: like in so many other ways, our modern society has made sex, and the relationship between the sexes, more complex and stressful instead of more fun and joyous. Studies keep showing that in our society, the level of impotence in men and sexual dysfunction in women is on the rise, so to speak. More than half of all marriages now end in divorce. Why is it that men and women are having such a difficult time with one another? Could it be because we're trying to dismiss the imperatives that are programmed into our bodies and our brains instead of respecting them and dealing with them?

I'm not about to make the case that we should ignore the strides made to bring equality to the sexes, trust me. The last hundred years have been a boon to society and in particular to women, who are finally approaching equanimity with men in many, many ways.

But by the same token I think that we need to pay attention to, and respect, the differences between us. Our biological brains are a thousand years behind Susan Faludi.

Men still, in the brains they were given at birth, crave being the hunters. They want to go out into the world, bag the biggest prize, bring it home, be worshipped for doing so, and then take a nice long nap.

Women still, in the brains they were given at birth, crave nurturing others, communication, emotional bonding, and creating a home.

But the messages sent by our society tell us that to honor those cravings is to live too limited a life; that in order to be a fully-realized person, you have to do it all. You need to go out in the world, be admired for having a wonderful career, be an effective communicator, and be emotionally available and present. You must know how to nurture others, you must be a warm and loving parent, you must make a perfect home.

How exhausting!

Of course we're furious at one another! We all know that the previous generation had it easier—not only in the business world where they worked hundreds of fewer hours a year, but also at home where the roles were much more clearly delineated and, therefore, manageable. It's no surprise that the last thing we want to do is make love to one another. None of us really understands our role anymore, and the current

> TODAY, 63 PERCENT OF WOMEN WITH CHILDREN UNDER THE AGE OF THREE HAVE JOBS OUTSIDE THE HOME. IN 1969, IT WAS 23 PERCENT.

generation is really feeling the brunt of the sexual confusion.

I hear it over and over from both women and men. Men admit that they don't feel sexual when they're not doing things that they consider "masculine" pursuits. They're turned on sexually when they come home from a day at the office, having won some major deal or client, and their lover is waiting there to congratulate them and admire them. That makes them feel strong and confident and effective in life, and that power carries over to the bedroom.

Women, often, feel turned on when they are well cared for: when someone is interested in their feelings, in how they look, in listening to what they have to say. They want to feel nurtured and pampered. Feeling potent in the boardroom does not usually translate into sexual excitement.

When the roles are unclear and complicated, there is stress.

Ours is the first generation that is dealing with it. **We've got to learn to cut ourselves a break.**

We're constantly fighting our own inner patterning; we know on a conscious and societal level that much of what we feel may be irrational, but we still boil with confusion and rage.

Men will often feel fury over the fact that in their heads they still carry the burden of hunting for the family's food (even if it's not necessarily true)—and yet they're ridiculed if they don't also do a major part of the nurturing and gathering. **It's just too much** (particularly when they can only focus on one thing at a time . . .).

And women will often feel a similar fury over the fact that they carry the primary responsibility for raising the family and nurturing the household—yet they're ridiculed if they don't also earn a significant salary and develop a satisfying career. **It's just too much.**

Since deep in our heads we still believe that the other sex should be taking a big part of the burden of life off our hands, we find ourselves more and more furious at one another and separate from each other.

It was supposed to be the opposite! Equality was supposed to bring us all together, make us each more fulfilled by living a more complete, richer life. Finally, women could have careers and men could actively participate in their children's lives.

What went wrong?

The problem is that we're all expecting too much of ourselves too quickly. Not only can't we overcome the natural patterning of our brains so easily, we're trying to rewrite the rules faster than our society will allow them to be rewritten. Sure, it would be great if we could all have half-time careers and use the other half of our time doing the nurturing and gathering. But no one offers half-time careers. So we all do full-time careers (indeed, full-time careers that take an average of 30 percent more of our time than thirty years ago). That means that the other critically important jobs

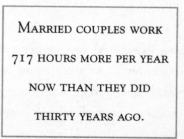

MARRIED COUPLES WORK 717 HOURS MORE PER YEAR NOW THAN THEY DID THIRTY YEARS AGO.

of running a household and maintaining a family have to be squeezed in alongside our stressful work lives, adding more stress and less time for everyone. Who's got the time to bring in the dry cleaning and do the grocery shopping and write out the monthly bill payments, much less deal with dropping kids off at school and hockey practice and talking to teachers and making sure everyone is eating healthy meals? All that, which our grandparents believed was someone's full-time job, is now delegated to the spare moments we can squeeze out from our career duties. Instead of readjusting the rules of society to accommodate the fact that we now value equality, our society is simply demanding that everyone do everything all the time. We don't each do half the task half the time; we do both tasks all the time.

Is it any wonder we don't have any time or desire to make love to one another?

There's yet another reason that I think men and women have been having problems with sex lately. **We know too much.**

Listen, our grandparents had sex (although I'm not completely sure my grandmother knew she was having it). Obviously they did, or we wouldn't be here! But nobody knew anything about it. We didn't hear the details of their sex lives. And they didn't talk about it. There were no books on the subject, the magazines didn't write about it. It was believed to be something private and personal. Today, nothing about sexuality is considered private.

We go to the movies and watch the most magnificent specimens of the human race doing to each other everything we could possibly imagine (and, frankly, often *more* than some of us could imagine!). I don't know about you, but after watching Brad Pitt prancing around naked in *Thelma and Louise*, it was a little disappointing to go home and watch my husband shuffle around in his slippers and flannel pajamas.

We read about sex. God, do we read about sex. We read about it until we're blue in the face, much less the genitals. Pick up any mainstream magazine for men or women, and there is at least one article telling us what we could be doing better in bed.

In the men's magazines the articles are characteristically male. Find the prey and kill it. Sex is treated as yet another task to be well performed with as little room for embarrassment, and as much room for adoration, as possible. A typical article: "How to Hit a Home Run Every Time: Finding the Clitoris, and Five Things to Do with It Once You Find It."

In the women's magazines, the focus is softer, of course, more often about communication and closeness: almost always more about the man's pleasure than the woman's. In fact, it's kind of amazing to me how many articles I see in those magazines that tell women what they need to do to give a man an erection. "Fifty Ways to Turn Him On in Bed," "How to Arouse Your Man and Keep Him Aroused," "A Hundred and One Tricks for Getting a Man Interested."

I'm no Racquel Welch, and I'll tell you that in my experience, you don't need to read a book to figure out how to get that thing up. It's not that complicated, is it? Men don't need much. For most of them, the sight of a tree with a knot hole will do the trick.

But we have to read article upon article, book upon book, about how to do it right and how to be the best and how to have mind-blowing sex. There's a woman who's made a living giving seminars for women on how to please men sexually. She's even written a bestselling book on the subject. At the beginning of the class, she hands everyone a banana, and by the time they leave, those women have tasted every bit of that banana, and not on top of their Special K, if you get my drift.

Now, could you imagine my grandmother taking such a class?

Look, I'm all for people having an active and imaginative sex life. There's nothing better than sex to keep you sane and happy and to reduce stress. It's good for the heart, the lungs, the muscles, and just about every other body part you've got. The mind, most of all.

> SEX IS A PRETTY SIMPLE ACT. DOES IT REALLY NEED THE THOUSANDS UPON THOUSANDS OF PAGES OF INSTRUCTIONS WRITTEN ABOUT IT EVERY YEAR?

But, these books and movies, and all the stuff we read and hear about sex day in and day out, is just nuts. It's unrealistic. Instead of encouraging us to use our senses, intimacy and imaginations to experiment with our partners and have a fulfilling sex life, it causes us anguish, pressure and unhappiness. Let's face it, how many of us have the perfect body or the perfect sex organ or the perfect technique for achieving the perfect orgasm that we read about in these books and magazines and see in the movies?

Anybody out there?

No? I thought so. But, of course, we keep reading and watching these things, because sex is fun. Advertisers and movie studios and publishers know that, so they keep giving us more and more and they keep making the details more and more intimate and titillating. Remember that scene in *Fatal Attaction* when Michael Douglas picks up Glenn Close and makes love to her while she's sitting in the sink? What the hell was that? And were those yells of pleasure coming out of her mouth really just the sound of someone with a fork stabbing into her butt?

While on some level watching sexual acrobatics may turn us on, ultimately the effect is de-

> ### The Tombstone No One Wants #7
>
> HERE LIES JANE DOE.
>
> HAS READ EVERY INTIMATE
>
> DETAIL OF HOW TO HAVE
>
> THE PERFECT SEX LIFE.
>
> NEVER FOUND AN
>
> ACCEPTABLE PARTNER.

pressing and isolating. Most of us end up feeling insecure and unhappy about ourselves. We've never had seventeen multiple orgasms, what's wrong with us? We don't have breasts like Sophia Loren—who's going to love us? We never knew a man who could really do it all night long. Are we the only ones missing all the fun?

I tried practicing my technique on a banana, but you know what? I bit the tip off by mistake. Now what?

The sex lives that are presented to us in books and magazines and movies and other media are more often than not complete fantasies. They are there to titillate and to excite and to sell product. They don't have to be based on anything that real people do behind locked doors.

But the effect is insidious and subtle. Just like the effect of too much advertising is to make us feel unhappy with the shabby old things we own, the effect of too much reading about sex is to make us feel like we must be inadequate. After all, *we're* not having the kind of sex that we see in the movies and read about in the magazines. We've bought our copy of *101 Nights of Grrrreat Sex* and you know what? It still wasn't so grrrrreat.

Because of this phenomenon, because we've all read and heard so much about the sex lives of the toned and perfect, sex has become a performance sport for many people. We measure ourselves against our competitors and against ourselves; we always are going for our personal best. *Cosmo says a woman can have five orgasms in a row and I'm damn well going to do it!*

Think about the fact that these days the phrase "good in bed" is a completely common term. You hear it constantly, and read about it everywhere, even in respectable newspapers and magazines. "He's no brain surgeon, but he's good in bed." Whether or not someone

> WHETHER OR NOT MY GRANDMOTHER WAS GOOD IN BED WAS NOT A TOPIC FOR CONVERSATION. IT WAS NOT SOMETHING ANYONE WOULD HAVE EVEN *thought* ABOUT!

is "good in bed" is discussed as readily and easily as whether or not they have good SAT scores.

Think of the pressure that comes along with that. Now, people know that their sexual performance is a matter for public consumption. So every time a young couple decides to finally sleep together, the level of worry and concern is tenfold what it used to be. Exposing yourself sexually is scary—and it always has been. But in the old days, at least we believed that when we did so, we were exposing ourselves only to one other person who cared about us. We had to overcome our insecurities about our bodies and about our performance, but at least we believed that what happened in that bedroom was intimate and private.

But now? We go into that bedroom not only insecure about our own attractiveness—but carrying with us all the stuff we've read and seen about sex. We're a walking sex manual: while we're getting to know each other's bodies, what used to be a joyous fumbling around and experimentation has become, for many people, yet another thing that we're being tested on, and that we can fail at.

This is it. This is the test. *Are you good in bed?* Show your stuff here, or be forever ridiculed among your peers.

So while you're trying to have fun, you're desperately trying to remember what that suggestion was you read in *Maxim* last week to help find the clitoris. Or you're holding the penis with exactly the proper light pressure, and holding it at the thirty-five-degree-angle-off-parallel that last month's *Cosmo* told you to. Why isn't it working? It must be because you don't look like Cindy Crawford.

Is it any surprise that people are complaining about sex these days? And that the chasm between the sexes seems to be wider than ever? There's so much pressure to perform associated with sex that more and more people are deciding it's all just too unpleasant.

So they're having anonymous cybersex instead. Now *there's* a way toward fulfilling spiritual intimate contact.

What to do?

First, we have to learn to respect the differences between the sexes. We don't have to like the fact that we're different, we don't have to succumb to the differences and live like the cavemen. But we have to respect that the differences exist. We have to understand that there are some things that women just should not expect a man to do. And there are some things that a man should realize are simply not in the woman's genetic makeup. Can those inclinations be overcome? Of course. But if we don't accept the fact that those inclinations exist, then we're bound to feel anger and rage over the fact that our partner just "doesn't get it."

We have to understand that there are certain things that we just shouldn't expect from the opposite sex. Women need to understand that when they say to a man "we have to talk" what he hears is "it's time for root canal." Men must understand that when they say to a women "but what's the point?" what she hears is "stop annoying me with how you feel."

⌖

We have to stop obsessing about our sexual perfor- mance, and just have fun. If you find yourself reading article after article about how to improve your sex life, and you find yourself drowning in the minute detail of what to touch, with how much pressure, for how long, at what angle, and with what exotic accompaniments, you know too much. You will lose the ability to be spontaneous and creative: get- ting ready to go to bed will feel like preparation for passing the bar exam.

I love the fact that in earlier generations when young people started to experiment with sex they called it "fooling around." Sex *should* be fooling around: it should be playful, it should be fun, it should be pressure-free. You shouldn't go into a sexual encounter worried about your performance or about how you measure up in the competitive arena.

If you are going into a sexual encounter with the

strong feeling that your partner is going to judge you on your comparative merits, and that instead of having fun you feel like you're competing for the gold medal in synchronized sex—get the hell out of there. Wait until you find someone with whom you can relax and enjoy it—someone who makes you feel appreciated just because you're there.

Sex is natural and exciting and fun. People have said that the great thing about sex is that even when it's bad, it's still pretty good. So why all the pressure? Why all the obsession over whether or not we're doing it perfectly, by the rules, as well as anyone has ever done it?

We have to put down the books and magazines and stop heaping pressure upon ourselves to "do it right" and just do it! Fumble around, make mistakes, be silly and be creative. Touch what you want to touch how you want to touch it, and tell your partner what you like and don't like.

Use sex as a way to communicate and enjoy the other person, not as a way to show off and bask in the narcissistic pleasure of your own performance. That keeps you distanced and alone.

Sex is about accepting the other person and accepting yourself—going into the situation naked as the day you were born, willing to just do what comes naturally. The best sex is uninhibited, spontaneous, unrehearsed. You need to put out of your head all the stuff you've read in those manuals: they get in the way of your staying present.

Try doing something really silly to break the pressure. Wear a funny hat. Do the hokey-pokey in the nude. Come to bed with rubber gloves and a plunger. Wear one of those surgical lights on your head.

Lighten up! You'll have much more fun.

Take a Socrates Break.
Don't ask me, ask yourself:

❖ *Does it make you angry that your partner doesn't have the same interests you do?*

❖ *How much time have you spent reading about sex rather than trying to actually do it with your partner?*

❖ *Have you compared your lover's looks or sexual performance to something you've seen in the movies? Favorably or unfavorably?*

❖ *Are you often angry because your mate doesn't fulfill the old-fashioned idea of what he or she should do? Why she doesn't cook and clean, and he doesn't bring home all the bacon?*

❖ *In the bedroom, do you go with what feels natural and fun, or do you find yourself resorting to techniques you once read about?*

❖ *Have you ever envied the sex life of a movie star? And just what makes you believe that it's so good?*

❖ *How often do you find yourself thinking: what the hell is he (she) talking about?*

❖ *Think about the one thing that drives you most crazy about your partner. Could it be, at least in part, due to biological patterning? If so, does that make it any easier to take?*

❖ *Does looking at photos of models make you feel bad because you don't look like that?*

❖ *Does sex feel joyous, or like another task you need to accomplish?*

8

Take Back Your Life!

On civility and community

A FEW MONTHS AGO I gave a seminar in Lansing, Michigan, on the subject of humor and optimism. When the program was over, a very well-dressed woman who looked to be in her mid-forties came up to me, and with a big open smile said, "Loretta, I'm so glad to finally be able to talk to you. I've come to see you six times."

"You've come to see me six times?"

"Yes."

I looked deeply in her eyes and said: "Well, for God's sake: Stop It!"

Of course, I love the fact that she found my lectures worth coming to again and again. But there's a concern that I felt I had to voice to her. If someone is coming to see me six times, then they may well be looking to me as if I have all the answers—as if I'm the guru who can show them the way to live. And I don't think anyone should look to gurus for the answers. Once we turn outside, looking to someone else as the "expert" who can give us the answers to how we live our lives, we're already on the wrong path.

There certainly are many things people can do to improve their lives, and many interesting thinkers and philosophers and coaches and trainers who can offer solid ideas and advice for living a more fulfilling life. But no one has all the answers for you. I don't know that anyone can even really know all the questions. We're all wonderfully and amazingly unique beings: each of us an exotic and special mixture of biological and psychological parts that make us whole.

Not a single one of us has exactly the same combination of hair color, eye shape, jaw line, cheek bones, muscle definition, leg length, toe shape, eyebrow density, and waist-to-hip ratio; not to mention our particular abilities to play the trombone, write a poem, climb a mountain, sing a ditty, dance the tango, understand quantum physics, nap on an airplane, giggle like a baby or paint the ceiling of the Sistine Chapel.

Who could possibly know all that you need, other than you? Who could possibly understand the particular mix of needs, dreams, fantasies and neuroses that make up your inner life?

So many of us today are searching for answers. We're looking for spiritual and practical ways to slow our lives down, to find a life that makes sense, to get rid of all of the crap that I've spent this book making fun of.

Many of us are turning to new religions, or going back to religions that we've left behind. Some of us are turning to more exotic and complex forms of spirituality. Many of us are reading books and going to seminars or weekend retreats to learn how to get in touch with our inner something or other.

We're all reading books on how to simplify our lives.

But for some of us, those spiritual searches lead to us feeling even more inadequate, and therefore full of stress and anxiety, than before. Even finding ways to calm down has become a big consumer business.

I don't know how many times I've had people say to me "Loretta, I know I should meditate, I know it would calm me down, but I don't know how."

The only reason someone would think that they don't know how to meditate is because they have made associations with meditation that are inaccurate. They think that they have to climb a mountain and wear robes and breathe jasmine incense and lock themselves up with nothing to eat but a cup of chamomile tea and some cilantro sprigs for weeks on end. They think they have to have the flexibility and muscle tone of Houdini and be able to stay in the lotus position for hours. They think they have to stand on their head and speak Farsi, or something like that, to do it properly.

People go to weekend retreats, and they read books that promise them the secret to happiness. "You can be happy all the time! Happiness is just a state of mind! It's all under your control!"

You can do anything, you can be anything you want to be, you can go as far as you can imagine. You can have unlimited power! The problem is not with the world, but with the way you see the world! You're in control!

So, of course, that makes us feel even more rage and self-hatred when life throws its normal disappointments and pain in our path. We aren't even left alone to feel unhappy without having the additional guilt laid upon our heads that it's our own fault for just not being more in control and more perfect. Your dog dropped dead? Your company fired you after fifteen years? How stupid of you to be sad about that! If you were a higher being, you wouldn't be so sad! You'd see this as an opportunity.

> MY GRANDMOTHER USED TO CLEAN OUT HER CLOSETS PERIODICALLY. THINGS SHE LIKED, SHE KEPT. THINGS SHE DIDN'T LIKE ANYMORE, SHE THREW OUT. SHE DID NOT NEED A BOOK TO TELL HER HOW.

We read books on how to "simplify our lives" and we see entries like "get rid of the boat" and "consolidate your investments." Well, excuse me: suppose we don't happen to have a boat, or even have investments? Again, the implication seems to be an accusation: it's your own fault that you're stressed; you have too many things.

We're told that if things at work aren't going the way we want them to go, it may just be that the *feng shui* in our workspace isn't exactly right. If you only knew that your desk should be facing the direction of the rising moon and that your fax machine needs a lot of open air and natural light, you wouldn't have these problems. But you didn't know that, did you? You're just not spiritually advanced enough. It's your fault.

In other words, if only you knew all the little esoteric rules of the world, if only you spent every free moment of your life learning all the details of all these arcane belief systems, then maybe you'd have the life you want.

Is it any wonder people go around shell-shocked and enraged? We've even made the search for fulfillment something that feels demanding and demoralizing.

Can I tell you something? It's normal to be sad sometimes. The *abnormal* thing is to be one of those people who walk around acting hap-hap-happy all the time. What the hell is that? Have they been lobotomized?

And you know what else? Life these days is enormously stressful and complicated and demanding. Cleaning out your closet to "simplify your life" is not going to go very far toward solving your problems unless your problem is a messy closet. Neither will you become a higher being by moving your couch from one side of the room to the other. It takes a whole lot more than that; but in a way, the real answer is so much more simple.

Each and every one of us has the ability to create a better life for himself, and it doesn't take a guru, it doesn't take self-help books, it doesn't take herbal supplements. All it takes is the ability to slow down, lighten up, think about what you're doing before you do it, and always, *ALWAYS*, choose the path that leads you towards a deeper connection with other people.

It's the need for community, the need to bond to other people, that our culture has ignored in favor of speed, convenience and workload. I'm often astounded that even among many of the groups that tout spirituality and healing and new-age pursuits, the emphasis is in the wrong place. Too often we are told as part of those programs that we have to look inward, we have to heal ourselves, we have to become more self-aware and self-actualized.

We're told *"you can't love another until you learn to love yourself."*

I think that is absolutely ridiculous. The truth is often just the opposite: **You can learn to love yourself by loving other people!** By becoming part of a larger group you can learn not only about your place in the world, but you can learn how much other people care about you, and therefore how worthy of love you are. How can you ever really feel

> LOOKING TOO HARD FOR SELF-ACTUALIZATION OFTEN LEADS TO SELF-ABSORPTION.

that you're lovable until there are many other people who love you? How can you really feel that you're worth caring about until there are many other people caring about you?

It's only when you're part of a thriving, intimate, intense community that you can understand and feel good about how worthwhile you are.

Human beings are tribal animals! We crave intimacy and connection. It's in the genes. Instant e-mail messaging just doesn't do it.

Years ago, a fascinating study was done in the town of Rosetto, Pennsylvania. Scientists were drawn there by the discovery that the incidence of heart disease was far lower than the national average, despite the facts that the largely Italian-American community ate a diet laden with fat and cholesterol, that a large percentage of the people smoked cigarettes, and that many of its men worked in the slate quarries two hundred feet below the earth.

During the course of the several-year study, scientists noted a marked rise in the rate of heart disease, despite no discernible change in the way that the people smoked, ate, worked, etc. Every aspect of their behavior was measured, and traditional medicine found no answers for the change in the level of heart disease.

Ultimately they came around to believing what many of us instinctively would know is true: the thing that kept these people healthy was the bond between them. When the study began, Rosetto was a town in which several generations of families lived together in close quarters. It was a community that was stable, predictable, supportive, loving. Family and friends were a buffer to outside pressures.

By the end of the study, the younger generation began

moving out to seek their fortunes elsewhere. Suburban sprawl invaded; fences were being built as quickly as superstores and satellite dishes dotted the town. As the stress of the outside world became more a part of daily life and the buffer of the closely-knit families disappeared, the rate of heart disease skyrocketed.

In another study, Dr. David Spiegel of Stanford University found that breast cancer patients who participated in close-knit support groups lived an average of **twice** as long as those who did not.

We need other people; we need close relationships and community and family not only for our psychological health, but for physical health, too. It's been proven that married people live longer than single people; and that in the three-year period following a heart attack, patients who are socially isolated are twice as likely to die than those with social interactions.

We need rich, rewarding, involved social communities for psychological and for physical health.

Look around; you know that this is true. Everywhere we turn, we see people crying out for some form of community. We see the incredible phenomenon of millions of people, sitting home alone, logging onto the Internet and joining "chat rooms" in which they type messages to one another, reaching out for connection. We see people logging on and watching websites in which cameras are mounted around other people's homes—and since there are no real people around whose lives they feel a part of, they watch the minute details of how other people eat their breakfast and put on pants. We watch television shows like *Survivor* and *Big Brother* in which groups of people are locked into some form of artificial community to-

WE SIT AT HOME, EACH MEMBER OF THE FAMILY IN A SEPARATE ROOM, EACH WATCHING A DIFFERENT FAMILY SITCOM!

gether, and we sit home alone, watching *them* learn the ins and outs of human interaction and negotiation. We watch people confronting their psychological, family and relationship issues on national television talk shows like *Jerry Springer*—but in an electronic and cynical form that is set up for broadcast, and that often leads to fisticuffs and has, at least twice, lead to real-life offscreen murder.

It couldn't be clearer. We're missing real human connection. We don't necessarily know that we're missing it, and in fact, most of us think that the way we live is pretty darn civilized—with no one ever knocking on our door, with people calling us when they know our machine will be the only one home, when no one is able to see us until three weeks from Tuesday. It seems to us that the way our grandparents lived lacked privacy and invaded personal boundaries. These days, who would stand for a life like they had? Doors open all the time, people running in and out; family gatherings at least once a week and often more than that; big family rituals that gathered the extended family and friends together several times a year; groups of neighbors always congregating in the kitchen, chatting and complaining and fussing and gossiping and just being, well, people. It's so messy and invasive.

And, yes, perhaps the way our grandparents did it was unsophisticated and occasionally disrespectful of limits, and sometimes, if not often, really just plain annoying and intrusive.

But the fact that they had people around them all the time made their lives saner. They were involved in the rich stories of the people around them, the people whose lives they could actually touch. The inbred craving to be part of those lives, to hear those stories, hasn't gone away—we just satisfy the craving with the antiseptic and anesthetized versions we see on TV.

We are one great enormous community of human beings, and the only thing that really brings richness to life is our connection with others. And the more people we are connected to, the more richness we can call on.

We're so busy these days that we set severe limits on who we will spend our time with. We tend to believe that every relationship we have needs to bring value with it—as if every personal encounter is a business dealing. *I'll spend time with you if you bring something good to the table.* We look at our relationships as commodities: if we are no longer getting what we want from other people, we discard them and move on to the next. Like sweaters from the Gap.

But if you ask me, the thing that is great about human relationships is that you never know where the value is going to come from. You never know when the surprise insight will come your way—or from whom. At any minute of any day, another person may touch your life with a moment of laughter, joy, pathos, friendship, intelligence, rage, fear or pure love.

Intensity of life comes from those moments. And yes, while my grandmother may have spent too much time around the kitchen table with her yenta friends minding other people's business, those conversations were intense, they were personal, and they were wildly intimate. Those ladies knew every detail of each other's lives—and the lives of each of their family members. The husbands would have been mortified if they had known!

And while much of the advice thrown around that table may not have been helpful, and may not have been clinically accurate, and may even have been downright unsophisticated and dumb, it gave the women something else, something much bigger than the value of the individual pieces of advice. It gave them an open forum in which to talk about what was bothering them. It gave them many differing opinions and therefore options to consider concerning whatever it was that they were talking about.

And most importantly, it showed them that other people **cared.** Other people were **there for them.** Other people **wanted to help.**

Today, so many people go to see therapists and coaches and join support groups to get the same kind of validation and caring that our ancestors got around their kitchen tables. And while those sorts of clinical experiences are very helpful, they don't replace a broad and rich range of intimate human connections. As wonderful and as supportive as they may be, they still take place only within prescribed boundaries. You see your therapist for one hour a week on Wednesdays at three. You see your support group on Monday nights.

We need to fill our lives with untidy, invasive, knock-on-the-door-unexpected relationships that help prove to us, every minute of the day, that we are cared for. We need to fill up our lives with people, PEOPLE! In all their shapes and sizes and with all their neuroses and hysteria and inappropriateness. We need to spend our days knocking back and forth with others, no matter how wonderful or how mundane the encounters. It is the encounters themselves that make life more interesting.

We've got to do everything we can to rejoin the human community, to connect ourselves to the people around us in ways that allow us to be truly touched. We must allow ourselves to become part of the messy, inefficient, sometimes unpleasant, sometimes wonderful, but always intense and engaging world of humanity.

It's only when we really open ourselves up, figuratively opening the doors and letting everyone into our kitchens, that we can appreciate not only what a luminous place the world is, but how important a part we play in it.

It's not easy, but there are many ways we can open ourselves up to the world around us, ways that were obvious (if not obligatory) in our grandmothers' world.

The first step, and perhaps the step that could really

take us in the direction that we all want to go, is for us to relearn the simple but profound art of basic human civility.

To me, civility is the most profound and basic form of spirituality. It's a spirituality that respects that we're all here, on Earth, in the same basic form, dealing with the same basic stuff; and that we all, each and every one of us, are deserving of respect and attention.

Yet, there are things about basic civility and manners that we have forgotten in these self-absorbed times. In my business I often speak at big new-age centers and conventions, and I have literally run into people who talk about "loving everyone unconditionally"—but never stop to say good morning! Maybe I'm nuts, but I think you've got to stop and be polite to someone before you can love them unconditionally.

People think this is a joke, but I know of a major figure of new-age thinking, someone who preaches love and understanding, who has it written into his speaking contracts that the limo driver who picks him up at the airport is restricted from speaking to him.

This is another "duh." Basic human decency and courtesy is a prerequisite. That's the foundation upon which a more complex and insightful understanding of love and kindness can be based.

The list that follows may sound idiotic, but I worry that in the rush of modern life, many of us have forgotten the basics. Over the course of thousands of years, human civilization has developed basic rules of behavior—and despite the fact that in our fast-paced, high-tech world, they feel a little shopworn and quaint—they still work, and they're still of vital importance. In order to make the world a better place, and a place in which you can start to build secure bonds with others, always remember the little things, things like:

- *Say "thank you" whenever someone does something for you even remotely worthy of it. Even if you pay them for it.*

- *Say "hello" whenever you see someone you know. And if you dare, even when you see someone you don't know.*

- *Say "goodbye" when you leave.*

- *Don't interrupt while others are talking.*

- *Let others go first.*

- *Say "excuse me."*

- *Wait your turn.*

- *Clean up after yourself (and your dog!).*

- *Never scream—even (or especially) at your kids.*

- *Be punctual.*

- *If you take the last cup of coffee, make a fresh pot.*

- *Say "Bless you," or "Gesundheit" when someone sneezes.*

❖ *Stand up and give a seat to the elderly, and to pregnant women.*

❖ *Don't talk in theaters.*

The basic rules of civility may seem like foolish old-fashioned schoolmarm regulations, but in fact what they accomplish is to build the foundation for more substantial relationships. When you abide by these rules, it paves the way for others to feel welcomed and for communication to begin. When you ignore these rules, others feel unwelcome and even disliked.

Civility is the freshman course. It's taking a seat behind the wheel. The more advanced lesson is in finding ways to not only put the car on the road, but to get it out on the highway.

You want to find ways to invite people in, to make them feel part of your life and to make you feel part of theirs. You want to give yourself the opportunity to feel the bond of Grandma Francesca's kitchen, where people said whatever was on their mind, and stopped over whenever they were in the mood.

Now, of course, in today's world no one is going to go back to an open screen door and a house full of neighbors. The goal is to re-create the emotional connection by keeping the connections intense.

Intensity between human beings grows out of intimacy. And today's world has done everything possible to get in the way of intimacy. You can't be intimate with answering machines; you can't be intimate when it takes a month to see your friends; you can't be intimate when you're constantly interrupted.

In its most basic form, intimacy takes *access*. If you're not physically available to allow for closeness, there's no way for closeness to develop. And, sadly, because of the way our culture has developed over the last few decades, simple access is hard to come by. Reclusiveness is the default for many, many people.

Here are a few ideas for how to help make yourself more open and accessible and available for intimacy:

❖ *If you're alone, answer your telephone.*

❖ *If you're with someone, don't answer the telephone.*

❖ *Cancel call waiting (Who are you waiting for, anyway?).*

❖ *If you miss a call, call back as soon as you can.*

❖ *Instead of meeting people at restaurants, invite them into your home and cook them a meal.*

❖ *Talk to strangers on airplanes.*

❖ *Make room for people you care about. If someone wants to see you, squeeze them into your schedule, no matter how tight it is. If you're too booked up with events to have them over for dinner, meet them for a cup of tea on Saturday afternoon, or stop for breakfast together on the way to work.*

❖ *If there's an illness or death among your neighbors or co-workers, pay a visit.*

❖ *Do a kindness without asking for, or expecting, a return.*

❖ *Pay someone a compliment, but it's got to be the truth.*

❖ *Never cancel an appointment. If you absolutely must, send a gift to apologize.*

❖ *Talk to people on elevators. When everybody is silent, everybody's feeling ridiculous. You'll be the hero by talking.*

❖ *Make at least one true intimate friend at work. Invite him or her over for dinner often. He or she will be your reality check at the workplace.*

❖ *Take a class in something you feel passion for.*

❖ *Volunteer.*

Fight the urge toward privacy. It's overrated! Privacy leads to isolation, and isolation leads to loneliness. And when we're lonely we tend to do whatever we can to fill the void. Like buy ten more shirts we don't need. Or watch Richard Hatch and John Wayne Bobbitt fight it out on *The Jenny Jones Show.*

The only thing that will really fill the void is when you build your own community.

And think about this: what almost always happens when you get a group of people together? Do you ever see a group of people sitting around, acting morose together? No. You see laughter, you see boisterous behavior, you see people having fun and telling jokes and being silly with one another.

The human animal is an amazing construction: it has the capacity to laugh, to make fun of itself, to be playful and to be funny. And think of how extraordinary that phenomenon is; what other animals do you see out there having a good time? You don't see dogs and cats slapping their knees, now do you?

But our biology craves it, because our biology is such that without laugher, we start to become ill. Without laughter, our blood pressure rises and our immune system becomes more vulnerable. Without laughter, we start to take ourselves way too seriously and the next thing you know, road rage sets in.

A recent study of happiness conducted by Dr. David Lykken of the University of Minnesota seems to indicate that, for the most part, we human beings are each born with our own individual capacity for feeling happiness. Whether we win the lottery or lose a spouse, chances are that our happiness "set point" will not vary all that much in the course of our lives. The search for "happiness" through the attainment of something external—career success, wealth, beauty, consumer objects—seems to now have been proven by science to be pointless. It doesn't work.

I love this finding for many reasons, but probably most of all because it's almost exactly what Francesca said to us all of our lives. You won't find happiness by looking outside or by trying to attain wealth or status. You only find happiness at home.

What does seem to work to make us more happy are the little things: the smell of someone cooking you breakfast in the morning; the feeling of holding a child's hand; the magnificence of a perfect sunset; the sharing of laughter. It's those little things that make life worth living, and that can make us feel like happier human beings. The more we allow ourselves to enjoy those little things, the happier we become.

And the best way, always, to have wonderful little moments, is to share them with others.

Think of other people as vitamin supplements! Because, in fact, that's just what they are. Other people supplement our own natural internal resources; they give us strength, they give us clarity, they cure depression, they lower our blood pressure. And with these supplements, the more the better! Take all you want, whenever you want.

Instead of St. John's Wort, which they say is good for depression, take an hour with your friend Ruby who makes you laugh! Instead of ginseng, which they say is good for vitality levels, spend half an hour at the park with your friend Kevin the jock. Instead of taking hops, which they say is good for a lack of appetite, invite a few friends over, spend some time in the kitchen preparing a sumptuous and satisfying meal, and share an evening of community, friendship and food.

You'll feel better. I guarantee it.

Notes

7 Martin Seligman, *Learned Optimism* (New York: Pocket Books, 1998).

9 Deidre Donahue, "And Now a Few Words About Those Sponsors: Sick of advertising everywhere, young America counterattacks U.S. companies' 'global culture,' " *USA Today*, April 4, 2000.

24 Joseph P. Kahn, "Generation Excess," *Boston Globe Magazine*, December 26, 1999, p. 14.

34 David Weeks and Jamie James, *Eccentrics: A Study of Sanity and Strangeness*, New York: Villard Books, 1995.

44 "Oprah talks to Elie Weisel," *O, The Oprah Magazine*, November 2000.

53 Elizabeth Olson, "Americans Lead the World in Hours Worked," *New York Times*, September 7, 1999.

62 Ellen Leibernluft, M.D., "Circadian Rhythms Factor in Rapid-Cycling Bipolar Disorder," *Psychiatric Times*, May 1996.

62 "Time of Day Medicine Dose Is Taken May Boost Its Efficacy, Cut Toxicity," *JAMA.* 275(1): 1996, pp. 143–44.

62 James B. Maas, *Power Sleep*, New York: Villard Books, 1999.

62 William C. Dement, *The Promise of Sleep*, New York: Delacorte Press, 1999.

66 Diane A. Riordan and Donna L. Street, "Type A behavior in the workplace: the good, the bad and the angry," *Strategic Finance*, 81(3), pp. 28–32.

67 David B. Posen, M.D. "Stress Management for Patient and Physician," *Canadian Journal of Continuing Medical Education*, April 1995.

67 Earle Holland, "Stress May Increase Susceptibility to Infectious Disease," *Ohio State University Research News*, July 23, 1999.

67 K. A. Matthews et al., "Does Stress Cause Carotid Atherosclerosis in Women?" *CardioConsult Reviews*, September 1998.

67 Sean Swint, "Level of Mental Stress May Help Doctors Predict Heart Attack," *WebMD Medical News*, December 8, 1999.

74 American Heart Association, "Biostatistical Fact Sheet on physical inactivity," AHA website, October 2000.

75 Jim Thornton, "Cheat and Run," *USA Weekend*, July 16, 2000.

77 Judy Putnam, "U.S. Food Supply Providing More Food and Calories," *Food Review*, October 1999.

77 "Obesity: A Major Risk Factor," Mayo Clinic. Web article, June 1, 1998.

79 Ross E. Anderson Ph.D., "Exercise, an Active Lifestyle and Obesity," *Physician and Sportsmedicine*, October 1, 1999, p. 41.

83 Jim DeBrosse, "Weighty Problems as Americans Grow Fatter," *The News and Observer* (Raleigh, NC), February 9, 1997, p. A21.

83 Jane E. Brody, "Planning Healthier Suburbs: Where Cars Sit Idle and People Get Moving," *New York Times*, October 17, 2000, p. F6.

84 Michael D. Jensen and James A. Levine, "Role of nonexercise activity thermogenesis in resistance to fat gain in humans," *Science*, Jan. 8, 1999, pp. 212–14.

90 Jane E. Allen, "No Minor Mix-Up," *Los Angeles Times*, January 10, 2000, p. S1.

108 Karen Auge, "Tighten Up Those Flabby Brains!" *Denver Post*, August 14, 2000, p. A01.

111 Don G. Campbell, *The Mozart Effect*. New York: Avon Books, 1997.

118 Karen Hayes, "Teenager Achieves Rare Feat: 4 Years Without TV," *Boston Globe*, April 2, 2000.

123 Joseph P. Kahn, "Generation Excess," *Boston Globe Magazine*, December 26, 1999.

127 Alexis Chiu, "As Candles Rise in Popularity, So Do Candle Fires, Deaths," The Associated Press, January 7, 1999.

175 Allan and Barbara Pease, *Why Men Don't Listen And Women Don't Read Maps*, New York: Welcome Rain Publishing Co., 2000.

207 Ron Grossman and Charles Leroux, "A New 'Roseto Effect'; 'People Are Nourished By Other People,' " *Chicago Tribune*, October 11, 1996.

207 Geoffrey Cowley with Anne Underwood, "Is Love the Best Drug?" *Newsweek*, March 16, 1998.

208 D. Spiegel, J. R. Bloom et al., "The Effect of Psychosocial Treatment on Survival of Patients with Breast Cancer," *Lancet*, October 14, 1989, pp. 888–91.

For information about Loretta LaRoche's seminars, presentations, and performances, please call 508-476-3998

Visit www.stressed.com.

For a free product catalog, call 1-800-99TADAH

ABOUT THE AUTHOR

An international consultant and lecturer in the field of stress management for more than twenty years, **Loretta LaRoche** is the author of *Relax—You May Only Have a Few Minutes Left*. Her five PBS specials and motivational videos have all been critically acclaimed bestsellers. She is an adjunct faculty member of the Mind/Body Medical Institute in Boston, which is affiliated with Care Group/Beth Israel and Harvard Medical School.